WRINKLIES™
Worldly Wit
& Wisdom

First published in Great Britain in 2009
This edition published 2018 by Prion
an imprint of the Carlton Publishing Group
20 Mortimer Street
London W1T 3JW
2 4 6 8 10 9 7 5 3 1

A catalogue record for this book is available
from the British Library

ISBN 978-1-91161-013-7

Typeset by e-type, Liverpool
Printed in Dubai

WRINKLIES™ Worldly Wit & Wisdom

Classic Quotes and Amusing Observations for the More Mature Members

Allison Vale & Alison Rattle

PRION

To my amazing Mum, the loveliest wrinkly I know.
Forever young to me.
A.R.

To my Dad, living proof there's nothing
wrinkly about being sixty!
A.V.

Contents

Introduction

The human race is unique in its enlistment of grandparents into the work of rearing the young. Studies among indigenous tribes have proven that the presence of a grandmother within the family unit will greatly improve the survival rates of any children. This gives the human race an advantage over all other species, for improved survival rates lead to greater longevity, which in turn leads to more grandparents and so on and so on.

This means that we have the audacious luck to live for twice as long as our nearest relative, the chimpanzee. The poor old female chimp expires shortly after she loses her fertility, while the human female could enjoy up to 50 years plus following the end of her fertile years. What a bonus!

Life for the over 50s has never been better. Women can now expect to live well into their 80s with men following close on their heels. This has given birth to an anti-ageing fad which takes full advantage of this spectacular longevity. The cross-over from adulthood into old age is becoming progressively blurred. With the growing popularity and acceptability of cosmetic surgery, many people now choose to deny the ageing process altogether (some with more success than others: Sharon Osbourne looks sensational, not so Jackie Stallone).

We must not forget that the autumn years serve their own purpose and should be embraced. There is an African proverb that illustrates beautifully how other cultures elevate age: 'The death of an old person is like the loss of a library.' Western societies are losing sight of this like never before. From both sides of the Atlantic we risk being overwhelmed by the new cult of celebrity. It is an inexhaustible quarry: periodically, someone sees fit to carve out another vacuous wannabe, bursting with youth, sex appeal and a psychotic need for fame. Often, talent is an irrelevance. Anyone willing to play strip poker live on national TV, eat unimaginable grubs in an Australian jungle, or disgrace themselves on a TV talent show, can grab their fleeting 15 minutes. Comedy baby naming is even turning the offspring of celebrities into readymade mini-celebrities. It's so dreary.

In truth, growing old is not what it used to be. Thanks to huge advances in medical science and the propensity of the media to bombard us with sleek visions of ageless, airbrushed celebrities, breaking the age barrier is easier than ever. Whoever now thinks of 50 or even 60 as being particularly old? Mick Jagger with his pants pulled over his belly; Joan Collins in wrinkled support tights? Not likely! Our healthier lifestyles and the invention of lycra undergarments have driven the physical signs of ageing back at least a decade. Look around any pub, theatre or nightclub, and you'll be sure to see plenty of vintage verve. The silver set are out there grabbing life by the throat as much, if not more, than the younger generation.

So, it is time we stop dishing out lifetime achievement awards that pay quiet lip service to 50-plus talents as we brush them aside. The names in this collection have energy, vibrancy and longevity. Retirement, for many of them, is out of the question.

This compilation celebrates the geniuses and giants of our time. The kind of professional entertainers who can still pull together three generations of a family around the TV and guarantee that everyone's laughing. The heavyweight actors

Introduction

who have put in decades of graft and now lend an emotional depth and gravitas to any scene. We challenge the stereotypes that this cult of celebrity would have us adopt: many here are sexy, sassy and sophisticated seniors who are still smouldering on screen and can give any skimpily clad 'artiste' something to wail about. Laugh along with Woody Allen, John Cleese, Julie Walters, Whoopi Goldberg and more, as they observe life's joys, trials and irritations.

The wrinkly years are not to be denied, reviled or feared, but to be welcomed and enjoyed. Forget a quiet, dignified old age and party on!

Growing Old is...

...when 'getting lucky' means finding your car in the car park.

...when an 'all nighter' means not getting up to pee.

...when 'getting a little action' means you don't need to eat any fibre.

...when you're told to slow down by the doctor instead of the police.

...when going bra-less pulls all the wrinkles out of your face.

...when a sexy babe catches your attention and your pacemaker opens the garage door.

...when your friends compliment you on your new alligator shoes and you're barefoot.

...when your wife says, 'Let's go upstairs and make love,' and you answer, 'Honey, I can't do both!'

...when you remember when it cost more to run a car than to park it.

All Anonymous

…when you've met so many people that every new person you meet reminds you of someone else.

Ogden Nash

Youthful Thinking

I never felt that there was anything enviable in youth. I cannot recall that any of us, as youths, admired our condition to excess or had a desire to prolong it.

Bernard Berenson

Zeal, n. A certain nervous disorder afflicting the young and inexperienced.

Ambrose Bierce

Youth would be an ideal state if it came a little later in life.

Herbert Asquith

Youth is a wonderful thing. What a crime to waste it on children.

George Bernard Shaw

American youth attributes much more importance to arriving at driver's licence age than at voting age.

Marshall McLuhan

Youthful Thinking

When we are young we are slavishly employed in procuring something whereby we may live comfortably when we grow old; and when we are old, we perceive it is too late to live as we proposed.

Alexander Pope

It is better to waste one's youth than to do nothing with it at all.

Georges Courteline

I'm aiming by the time I'm 50 to stop being an adolescent.

Wendy Cope

I live in that solitude which is painful in youth, but delicious in the years of maturity.

Albert Einstein

Youth is like spring, an overpraised season.

Samuel Butler

Old age at least gives me an excuse for not being very good at things that I was not very good at when I was young.

Thomas Sowell

We are only young once. That is all society can stand.

Bob Bowen

When you are young, you want to be the master of your fate and the captain of your soul. When you are older, you will settle for being the master of your weight and the captain of your bowling team.

Anon

In youth we run into difficulties. In old age difficulties run into us.

Beverly Sills

You're only as old as you feel… but you can't be Shirley Temple on the Good Ship Lollipop forever. Sooner or later, damnit, you're old.

Joan Crawford

If youth knew; if age could.

Henri Estienne

Till Death Us Do Part

My wife and I were happy for 20 years. Then we met.

Rodney Dangerfield

I married the first man I ever kissed. When I tell this to my children they just about throw up.

Barbara Bush

Till Death Us Do Part

Some people ask the secret of our long marriage.
We take time to go to a restaurant two times a
week. A little candlelight, dinner, soft music and
dancing. She goes Tuesdays, I go Fridays.

Henny Youngman

My wife and I tried to breakfast together, but we had
to stop or our marriage would have been wrecked.

Winston Churchill

In mid-life the man wants to see how irresistible
he still is to younger women. How they turn their
hearts to stone and more or less commit a murder
of their marriage I just don't know, but they do.

Patricia Neal

When asked his secret of love, being married 54
years to the same person, he said, 'Ruth and I are
happily incompatible.'

Billy Graham

I've been in love with the same woman for 49
years. If my wife ever finds out, she'll kill me.

Henny Youngman

Ann Meara of the comedy team Stiller and Meara
observed a while ago in a *New York Times*
interview of her 30-plus year-marriage, 'Was it love
at first sight? It wasn't then – but it sure is now.'

Ann Meara

Till Death Us Do Part

You, that are going to be married, think things can never be done too fast: but we that are old, and know what we are about, must elope methodically, madam.

Oliver Goldsmith

No man or woman really knows what perfect love is until they have been married a quarter of a century.

Mark Twain

My new wife is 32 and I'm 70. She's rejuvenated me totally. It's so exciting to see life through the eyes of a modern girl.

Wilbur Smith

Sheila and I just celebrated our thirtieth wedding anniversary. Somebody asked her, what was our secret? She answered, 'On my wedding day, I decided to make a list of 10 of Tim's faults which, for the sake of our marriage, I would always overlook. I figured I could live with at least 10!' When she was asked which faults she had listed, Sheila replied, 'I never did get around to listing them. Instead, every time he does something that makes me mad, I simply say to myself, "Lucky for him, it's one of the 10!"'

Tim Hudson, Chicken Soup for the Romantic Soul

There is no greater happiness for a man than approaching a door at the end of a day knowing someone on the other side of that door is waiting for the sound of his footsteps.

Ronald Reagan

The other night I said to my wife Ruth, 'Do you feel that the sex and excitement have gone out of our marriage?' She said, 'I'll discuss it with you during the next commercial.'

Milton Berle

One Christmas my husband gave me a chenille hand-knitted bobble hat. It was like we'd never met. I opened it and I said, 'Did you not like me when you bought me this?'

Arabella Weir

I'd marry again if I found a man who had 15 million dollars, would sign over half to me, and guarantee that he'd be dead within a year.

Bette Davis

I've had an exciting time. I married for love and got a little money along with it.

Rose Fitzgerald Kennedy

We were just happy to be in the same room together.

Judi Dench, on her long marriage to Michael Williams

Till Death Us Do Part

Before marriage, a man will lie awake all night thinking about something you've said. After marriage, he'll fall asleep before you finish saying it.

Helen Rowland

I suppose when they reach a certain age some men are afraid to grow up. It seems the older the men get, the younger their new wives get.

Elizabeth Taylor

As you get older, you realise it's work. It's that fine line between love and companionship. But passionate love? I'd love to know how to make that last.

Tracey Ullman

All marriages are happy. It's trying to live together afterwards that causes all the problems.

Shelley Winters

Instead of getting married again, I'm going to find a woman I don't like and just give her a house.

Rod Stewart

The man or woman you really love will never grow old to you. Through the wrinkles of time, through the bowed frame of years, you will always see the dear face and feel the warm heart union of your eternal love.

Alfred A. Montapert

My husband, like most men, can only do one thing at a time. If there's two cups of tea to be made, they'll make one. And then they'll make another one after that. If my husband's going to the shop and I say, 'Can you get a loaf of bread and a pint of milk?' he'll come back with one or the other. Never both.

Linda Robson, Grumpy Old Women

Before marriage, a man will lay down his life for you; after marriage he won't even lay down his newspaper.

Helen Rowland

Marriage is like a cage; one sees the birds outside desperate to get in, and those inside desperate to get out.

Ogden Nash

The conception of two people living together for 25 years without having a cross word suggests a lack of spirit only to be admired in sheep.

Alan Patrick Herbert

Till Death Us Do Part

My wife Mary and I have been married for 47 years and not once have we had an argument serious enough to consider divorce; murder, yes, but divorce, never.

Jack Benny

Men have got no reason to be grumpy at all [at Christmas time], because they don't have to do anything. They really don't do anything. In fact, my husband goes out on Christmas Eve to buy my present. He's had 364 days to go and get it, and he goes on Christmas Eve.

Linda Robson, Grumpy Old Women

I never knew what real happiness was until I got married, and by then it was too late.

Max Kaufman

Bigamy is having one wife too many. Marriage is the same.

Oscar Wilde

That married couples can live together day after day is a miracle that the Vatican has overlooked.

Bill Cosby

After about 20 years of marriage, I'm finally starting to scratch the surface of that one. And I think the answer lies somewhere between conversation and chocolate.

Mel Gibson, when asked if he knew what women want

We do not squabble, fight or have rows. We collect grudges. We're in an arms race, storing up warheads for the domestic Armageddon.

Hugh Leonard

On my sixtieth birthday my wife gave me a superb birthday present. She let me win an argument.

Anon

Basically my wife was immature. I'd be at home in the bath and she'd come in and sink my boats.

Woody Allen

Women! I have no idea. I don't know anything about women at all. They're a complete mystery to me.

Bryan Ferry

I was married for 30 years. Isn't that enough? I've had my share of dirty underwear on the floor.

Martha Stewart

Your marriage is in trouble if your wife says, 'You're only interested in one thing,' and you can't remember what it is.

Milton Berle

There's one thing about a late marriage – it doesn't last long.

Elderly Irishman, talking on Irish TV about courting in the 1940s

A friend recently told us about a 25th anniversary party where the husband gave a toast and said, 'The key to our success is very simple. Within minutes after every fight, one of us says, "I'm sorry, Sally".'

Cokie and Steve Roberts

I haven't spoken to my wife in years. I didn't want to interrupt her.

Rodney Dangerfield

We are so fond of one another, because our ailments are the same.

Jonathan Swift

To see a young couple loving each other is no wonder, but to see an old couple loving each other is the best sight of all.

William Makepeace Thackeray

I swear there are drugs in the upholstery of his chair. Because honestly he just gets near the television and goes zzz… It's known as the drugged chair.

Dillie Keane, Grumpy Old Women

Sexy at Sixty

I know nothing about sex because I was always married.

Zsa Zsa Gabor

Before we make love my husband takes a pain killer.

Joan Rivers

The Three Ages of Marriage: 20 is when you watch the TV after. 40 is when you watch the TV during. 60 is when you watch the TV instead.

Anon

After a man passes 60, his mischief is mainly in his head.

Washington Irving

Men of my age are just too old, and the younger ones may have the energy but they don't have the intellect.

Cilla Black

You know you're getting older when you have sex with someone half your age and it's legal.

Dan Savage

Statistics show that at the age of 70, there are five women to every man. Isn't that the darnedest time for a guy to get those odds?

Anon

The longer thread of life we spin
The more occasion still to sin.

Robert Herrick

Sexy at Sixty

When a girl's under 21 she's protected by the law.
When she is over 65, she's protected by nature and
anywhere in between, she's fair game.

Cary Grant

What is a younger woman? I'm pretty old, so
almost every woman is younger than me.

Jack Nicholson

It seems that after the age of 50, I began to age at
the rate of about three years per year. I began
falling asleep 15 minutes into an episode of
Seinfeld. I also began falling asleep during sex rather
than after.

Anon

When they were asked what they thought of a
phone mast being erected on the adjacent military
museum, one 97-year-old raised his hand to ask,
'Will it make us sterile?'

General Sir Jeremy MacKenzie, referring to a Chelsea
pensioner

You still chase women, but only downhill.

Bob Hope, on turning 70

We look forward to a disorderly, vigorous, un-
honoured and disreputable old age.

Don Marquis

Sexy at Sixty

Old guys of 50-plus love me with a whip in my hand.

Anne Robinson

Every man over 40 is a scoundrel.

George Bernard Shaw

As you get older, you don't get as horny – I don't take as many cold showers a day as I used to.

Tom Jones

There will be sex after death, we just won't be able to feel it.

Lily Tomlin

You can live without sex but not without glasses.

Anon

At 70, I find orgasmic sex quite dispensable.

Tennessee Williams

75-year-old (celebrating his birthday in a brothel): I haven't had a woman in longer than I care to say. You know she doesn't have to be beautiful – just patient.

Polly Platt and Louis Malle

The pleasures that once were heaven, look silly at 67.

Noel Coward

Sexy at Sixty

Now that I'm over 60, I'm veering towards respectability.

Shelley Winters

I'm still a terrible flirt. It boosts your ego knowing you still have the ability, but that's as far as it goes. Now we have a silly rule – no hands in jumpers.

Antony Worrall Thompson

If you can't have fun as an ageing sex symbol when you hit 60, I don't know what will become of you.

Raquel Welch

I'm not a raver any more, all good things must come to an end.

Jack Nicholson

You don't get older, you get better.

Shirley Bassey

My wild oats have turned to shredded wheat.

Anon

How exciting! This is the first time I've ever been implicated in a sex case. I don't remember handling her breasts. We were just having lunch.

Antony Worrall Thompson, on being accused of having an affair

Mary Wesley has thick white hair, endless legs and the captivating face that made her such a sexy beauty in her youth. Next year she will be 90, which she finds rather irritating because there is nothing elderly about her.

Lynda Lee-Potter

My love life is terrible. The last time I was inside a woman was when I visited the Statue of Liberty.

Woody Allen

I have so little sex appeal that my gynaecologist calls me 'sir'.

Joan Rivers

Clinton lied. A man might forget where he parks or where he lives, but he never forgets oral sex, no matter how bad it is.

Barbara Bush

I'm a different guy here in my 60s. I don't have the same libido. It used to be that I didn't think I could go to sleep if I wasn't involved in some kind of amorous contact. Well, I spend a lot of time sleeping alone these days.

Jack Nicholson

In my next life I'm going to come back as a rather good-looking, even quite fat and plain 50-year-old man, who's just been widowed or sadly divorced, and I would go to the country and I would clean up. I would get a bonk every night of the week.

Jilly Cooper, Grumpy Old Women

Sexy at Sixty

Sex appeal is in your heart and head. I'll be sexy no matter how old or how my body changes.

Sonia Braga

One of the best parts of growing older? You can flirt all you like since you've become harmless.

Liz Smith

Getting older is all about high blood pressure, high cholesterol, high anxiety, and low sex drive. At my age, 'safe sex' is not falling out of bed.

Anon

It's been so long since I've had sex I've forgotten who ties up whom.

Joan Rivers

There are a number of mechanical devices which increase sexual arousal, particularly in women. Chief among these is the Mercedes-Benz 380SL convertible.

P.J. O'Rourke

I had wanted for years to get Mrs Thatcher in front of my camera… as she got more powerful she got sort of sexier.

Helmut Newton

In my outrageous 20s, I asked a charming, chatty Englishwoman I'd met in Villefranche when people stopped having sex. 'It's no good asking me, my dear,' she said. 'I'm only 83.'

Anon

I once had a rose named after me and I was very flattered. But I was not pleased to read the description in the catalogue: no good in a bed, but fine up against a wall.

Eleanor Roosevelt

I was with this girl the other night and from the way she was responding to my skilful caresses, you would have sworn that she was conscious from the top of her head to the tag on her toes.

Emo Philips

My grandmother's 90; she's dating a man 93. They never argue: they can't hear each other.

Cathy Ladman

Having sex at my age is still wonderful, really. It just gets more difficult to see with whom you are having it.

Anon

Viva Viagra

I only take Viagra when I am with more than one woman.

Jack Nicholson

Viva Viagra

Sex at the age of 84 is a wonderful experience. Especially the one in the winter.

Milton Berle

There is more money being spent on breast implants and Viagra than on Alzheimer's research. This means that by 2030, there should be a large elderly population with perky boobs and huge erections and absolutely no recollection of what to do with them.

Anon

At my age, I'm envious of a stiff wind.

Rodney Dangerfield

Everything that goes up must come down. But there comes a time when not everything that's down can come up.

George Burns

An elderly gentleman went to the local drugstore and asked the pharmacist for Viagra. The pharmacist said, 'That's no problem. How many do you want?' The man replied, 'Just a few, maybe half a dozen, but can you cut each one into four pieces?' The pharmacist said, 'That's too small a dose. That won't get you through sex.' The gentleman said, 'Oh, that's all right. I'm past 80 years old, and I don't even think about sex any more. I just want it to stick out far enough so I don't pee on my shoes.'

Anon

Viva Viagra

Look at Catherine Zeta-Jones and Michael Douglas. She's a clever girl, because like me, she knows that an older man has time to love and nurture you.

Celine Dion

Bob Dole revealed he is one of the test subjects for Viagra. He said on Larry King, 'I wish I had bought stock in it.' Only a Republican would think the best part of Viagra is the fact that you could make money off of it.'

Jay Leno

If I marry again at my age, I'll go on honeymoon to Viagra Falls.

George Burns

An elderly man goes to confession and says to the priest, 'Father, I'm 80 years old, married, have four kids and 11 grandchildren. I started taking Viagra and last night I had an affair and made love to two 18-year-old girls. Both of them. Twice.'

The priest said: 'Well, my son, when was the last time you were in confession?'

'Never, Father, I'm Jewish.'

'So then, why are you telling me?'

'Heck! I'm telling everybody!'

Anon

Old Women...

...will never wake you in the middle of the night to ask, 'What are you thinking?' They don't care what you think.

...look good in bright red lipstick, unlike younger women and drag queens.

...have lived long enough to know how to please a man in ways their daughters could never dream of.

...develop a well-honed sixth sense as they age. They instinctively know when you've goofed up.

...are genetically superior: for every spectacular babe of 70 there is a rotund and receding relic in yellow plaid pants flirting ridiculously with the 22-year-old waitress.

All Anonymous

...are best, because they always think they may be doing it for the last time.

Ian Fleming

Whenever I see an old lady slip and fall on a wet sidewalk, my first instinct is to laugh. But then I think, what if I was an ant, and she fell on me. Then it wouldn't seem quite so funny.

Jack Handey

...are like aging strudels – the crust may not be so lovely, but the filling has come at last into its own.

Robert Farrar Capon

Some turn to vinegar, but the best improve with age.

C.E.M. Joad

Time and trouble will tame an advanced woman, but an advanced old woman is uncontrollable by any earthly force.

Dorothy L. Sayers

What's more beautiful than an old lady with white hair, grown wise with age and able to tell lovely stories about her past?

Brigitte Bardot

There are three classes into which all the women past 70 that ever I knew were to be divided: 1. That dear old soul; 2. That old woman; 3. That old witch.

Samuel Taylor Coleridge

If you want a thing done well, get a couple of old broads to do it.

Bette Davis

Old Men...

...have so much more to offer than young guys. They've done all their running and sown all their wild oats.

Celine Dion

...fall asleep in the middle of television programmes for no apparent reason. In the middle of conversations actually, or is that just me? One minute there's an adult person you're engaging with on some vaguely cerebral level, and the next minute there's somebody quietly snoring.

Kathryn Flett, Grumpy Old Women

...can be short and dumpy and getting bald but if [they have] fire, women will like [them].

Mae West

...are only walking hospitals.

Wentworth Dillon

Old People

Old people don't need companionship. They need to be isolated and studied so it can be determined what nutrients they have that might be extracted for our personal use.

Homer Simpson

At the Harvest Festival in church the area behind the pulpit was piled high with tins of IXL fruit for the old-age pensioners. We had collected the tinned fruit from door to door. Most of it came from old-age pensioners.

Clive James

Old people do more scandalous things than any rebel you want to name. Because they don't give a damn. They couldn't give a rat's ass what you think. They're 80 years old. They're leaving soon, you know what I mean?

Chris Isaak

It would be a good thing if young people were wise, and old people were strong, but God has arranged things better.

Martin Luther

The great secret that all old people share is that you really haven't changed in 70 or 80 years. Your body changes, but you don't change at all. And that, of course, causes great confusion.

Doris Lessing

Generation Gap

One thing only has been lent to youth and age in common – discontent.

Matthew Arnold

Generation Gap

The young do not know enough to be prudent, and therefore they attempt the impossible – and achieve it, generation after generation.

Pearl S. Buck

Young men are apt to think themselves wise enough, as drunken men are apt to think themselves sober enough.

Philip Dormer

My generation, faced as it grew with a choice between religious belief and existential despair, chose marijuana. Now we are in our Cabernet stage.

Peggy Noonan

It's not catastrophes, murders, deaths, diseases, that age and kill us; it's the way people look and laugh, and run up the steps of omnibuses.

Virginia Woolf

It's all that the young can do for the old, to shock them and keep them up to date.

George Bernard Shaw

Actually, I think children should be taught to be bored. I was in a coma of boredom throughout the 70s. The shops weren't even open on a Sunday, and your nanna, both your nannas, came for lunch and you had to be there.

Jenny Eclair, Grumpy Old Women

Methuselah lived to be 969 years old. You boys and girls will see more in the next 50 years than Methuselah saw in his whole lifetime.

Mark Twain

One age blows bubbles and the next breaks them.

William Cowper

But it's hard to be hip over 30 when everyone else is 19, when the last dance we learned was the Lindy, and the last we heard, girls who looked like Barbra Streisand were trying to do something about it.

Judith Viorst

When I was as you are now, towering in the confidence of 21, little did I suspect that I should be at 49, what I now am.

Samuel Johnson

My mother is going to have to stop lying about her age because pretty soon I'm going to be older than she is.

Tripp Evans

The question that is so clearly in many potential parents' minds: 'Why should we stunt our ambitions and impoverish our lives in order to be insulted and looked down upon in our old age?'

Joseph A. Schumpeter

But no matter how they make you feel, you should always watch elders carefully. They were you and you will be them. You carry the seeds of your old age in you at this very moment, and they hear the echoes of their childhood each time they see you.

Kent Nerburn

The main thing wrong with the younger generation is that we aren't in it.

Anon

Sagacity

WISDOM

And in the end, it's not the years in your life that count. It's the life in your years.

Abraham Lincoln

All would live long, but none would be old.

Benjamin Franklin

There are compensations for growing older. One is the realisation that to be sporting isn't at all necessary. It is a great relief to reach this stage of wisdom.

Cornelius Otis Skinner

Despite my 30 years of research into the feminine soul, I have not yet been able to answer the great question that has never been answered: What does a woman want?

Sigmund Freud

No man loves life like him that's growing old.

Sophocles

Old age deprives the intelligent man only of qualities useless to wisdom.

Joseph Joubert

If a human is modest and satisfied, old age will not be heavy on him. If he is not, even youth will be a burden.

Plato

The older I grow, the more I listen to people who don't say much.

Germain G. Glidden

The more sand that has escaped from the hourglass of our life, the clearer we should see through it.

Anon

The man who views the world at 50 the same as he did at 20 has wasted 30 years of his life.

Muhammad Ali

Sagacity

Early to rise and early to bed. Makes a male healthy, wealthy and dead.

James Thurber

If you wait, all that happens is that you get older.

Mario Andretti

Everyone should keep a mental wastepaper basket and the older he grows the more things he will consign to it – torn up to irrecoverable tatters.

Samuel Butler

The thing you realise as you get older is that parents don't know what the hell they're doing and neither will you when you get to be a parent.

Mark Hoppus

As you get older, though, you realise there are fire extinguishers. You do have an ability to control the flames.

Chaka Khan

And you learn as you get older, you learn to play the pauses better.

Michael Parkinson

The older we grow the greater becomes our wonder at how much ignorance one can contain without bursting one's clothes.

Mark Twain

You can tell a lot about a fellow's character by his way of eating jellybeans.

Ronald Reagan

I'm very pleased with each advancing year. It stems back to when I was 40. I was a bit upset about reaching that milestone, but an older friend consoled me. 'Don't complain about growing old – many, many people do not have that privilege.'

Earl Warren

Many are saved from sin by being so inept at it.

Mignon McLaughlin

Life's under no obligation to give us what we expect.

Margaret Mitchell

You can't be brave if you've only had wonderful things happen to you.

Mary Tyler Moore

Wisdom doesn't necessarily come with age. Sometimes age just shows up all by itself.

Tom Wilson

Old age comes at a bad time.

San Banducci

Sagacity

We all take different paths in life, but no matter where we go, we take a little of each other everywhere.

Tim McGraw

Perhaps one has to be very old before one learns to be amused rather than shocked.

Pearl S. Buck

It takes about 10 years to get used to how old you are.

Anon

In three words I can sum up everything I've learned about life: it goes on.

Robert Frost

My father always used to say that when you die, if you've got five real friends, then you've had a great life.

Lee Iacocca

You see things; and you say, 'Why?' But I dream things that never were; and I say, 'Why not?'

George Bernard Shaw

Old age is life's parody.

Simone de Beauvoir

Sagacity

The end comes when we no longer talk with ourselves. It is the end of genuine thinking and the beginning of the final loneliness.

Eric Hoffer

Minds ripen at very different ages.

Elizabeth Montagu

To be 70 years young is sometimes far more cheerful and hopeful than to be 40 years old.

Oliver Wendell Holmes Jr.

The old believe everything;
The middle-aged suspect everything;
The young know everything.

Oscar Wilde

He who laughs most, learns best.

John Cleese

Wherever there is power, there is age. Don't be deceived by dimples and curls. I tell you that babe is a thousand years old.

Ralph Waldo Emerson

Error is acceptable as long as we are young; but one must not drag it along into old age.

Johann Wolfgang von Goethe

Sagacity

Adulthood is the ever-shrinking period between childhood and old age. It is the apparent aim of modern industrial societies to reduce this period to a minimum.

Thomas Szasz

Many talents preserve their precociousness right into old age.

Karl Kraus

All the world's a stage and most of us are desperately unrehearsed.

Sean O'Casey

What do I know of man's destiny? I could tell you more about radishes.

Samuel Beckett

Few people think more than two or three times a year; I have made an international reputation for myself by thinking once or twice a week.

George Bernard Shaw

If at first you don't succeed, failure may be your style.

Quentin Crisp

Honest criticism is hard to take, particularly from a relative, a friend, an acquaintance or a stranger.

Franklin P. Jones

70 per cent of success in life is showing up.

Woody Allen

If you can't convince them, confuse them.

Harry S. Truman

A positive attitude may not solve all your problems, but it will annoy enough people to make it worth the effort.

Herm Albright

Misers aren't much fun to live with, but they do make wonderful ancestors.

Anon

Past is past and we must live the present to survive the future.

Martin Ducavne

The future is assured. It's just the past that keeps changing.

Russian joke

May the best of your past be the worst of your future.

Anon

The past is history; the future is a mystery; this moment is a gift; that is why this moment is called the present; enjoy it.

Allan Johnson

Sagacity

Know what's weird? Day by day, nothing seems to change, but pretty soon… everything's different.

Calvin, Calvin and Hobbes

Imagination was given to man to compensate him for what he isn't. A sense of humour was provided to console him for what he is.

Horace Walpole

You were born an original. Don't die a copy.

John Mason

To be able to feel the lightest touch really is a gift.

Christopher Reeve

If women ran the world we wouldn't have wars, just intense negotiations every 28 days.

Robin Williams

If you think before you speak the other guy gets his joke in first.

Jimmy Nail

For a happy and successful life you need a love of people and a love of maths.

Johnny Ball

If you obey all the rules, you miss all the fun.

Katharine Hepburn

People always call it luck when you've acted more sensibly than they have.

Anne Tyler

You don't stop laughing when you grow old; you grow old when you stop laughing.

Anon

Women on Ageing

I have to be careful to get out before I become the grotesque caricature of a hatchet-faced woman with big knockers.

Jamie Lee Curtis

I shall not grow conservative with age.

Elizabeth Cady Stanton

No one can avoid ageing, but ageing productively is something else.

Katherine Graham

A woman my age is not supposed to be attractive or sexually appealing. I just get kinda tired of that.

Kathleen Turner

Women on Ageing

At last now you can be what the old cannot recall
and the young long for in dreams, yet still include
them all.

Elizabeth Jennings

When I passed 40 I dropped pretence, 'cause men
like women who got some sense.

Maya Angelou

A woman's always younger than a man at equal
years.

Elizabeth Barrett Browning

Old age, believe me, is a good and pleasant thing. It
is true you are gently shouldered off the stage, but
then you are given such a comfortable front stall as
spectator.

Jane Harrison

You couldn't live 82 years in the world without
being disillusioned.

Rebecca West, at age 82

I do resent that when you're in the most cool,
powerful time of your life, which is your 40s,
you're put out to pasture. I think women are so
much cooler when they're older. So it's a drag that
we're not allowed to age.

Rosanna Arquette

I am really looking forward as I get older and older, to being less and less nice.

Annette Bening

When you're young, you just go right along. When you're older, you think, they've switched the rules on me.

Linda Evans

You know, when I first went into the movies Lionel Barrymore played my grandfather. Later he played my father and finally he played my husband. If he had lived I'm sure I would have played his mother. That's the way it is in Hollywood. The men get younger and the women get older.

Lillian Gish

The older I get the more of my mother I see in myself.

Nancy Friday

You take your life in your own hands, and what happens? A terrible thing: no one to blame.

Erica Jong

I spend most of my time puffing up my ego… till I'm this big ego thing… but it doesn't take much for it to be pricked, and then I'm just this deflated, shrivelled, shamed old woman with a bit of wee running down my legs.

Jenny Eclair, Grumpy Old Women

Women on Ageing

I have become more vocal in my complaining. I now say, 'This is not working for me.' This is my new sentence… It's just letting them know it's all about you, and for you, it's not working.

India Knight, Grumpy Old Women

I do write a hell of a lot of letters of complaint. I haven't really got time to do it, but I find it gets rid of some of my rage.

Sheila Hancock, Grumpy Old Women

Life is more interesting. When you're self-involved and you see yourself centre stage all the time, you're in agonies of self-consciousness, you're really concerned: how do I look? How do I sound? It's wonderful not to care about that any more.

Germaine Greer

You end up as you deserve. In old age you must put up with the face, the friends, the health, and the children you have earned.

Fay Weldon

Do not deprive me of my age. I have earned it.

May Sarton

Being 70 is not a sin.

Golda Meir

Women on Ageing

One of the many things nobody ever tells you about middle age is that it's such a nice change from being young.

Dorothy Canfield Fisher

It is not all bad, this getting old, ripening. After the fruit has got its growth it should juice up and mellow. God forbid I should live long enough to ferment and rot and fall to the ground in a squash.

Emily Carr

As a lady of a certain age, I am willing to let the photographers and their zoom lenses stay, but only if they use their Joan Collins lens on me for close-ups.

Kay Ullrich

Every woman over 50 should stay in bed until noon.

Mamie Eisenhower

I've had to tone it down a bit. But I've still got fabulous legs and wear mini-skirts. I'll keep wearing bikinis till I'm 80… I will grow old gracefully in public – and disgracefully in private.

Jerry Hall

Men on Ageing

I don't want to be the oldest performer in captivity… I don't want to look like a little old man dancing out there.

Fred Astaire

When our memories outweigh our dreams, we have grown old.

Bill Clinton

That sign of old age, extolling the past at the expense of the present.

Sydney Smith

Men become old, but they never become good.

Oscar Wilde

As men get older, their toys get more expensive.

Marvin Davis

You get older and suddenly you don't have to go out and do all that sh*t you do when you're young and dumb. Because now you're old and dumb instead.

Johnny Depp

Old age, calm, expanded, broad with the haughty breadth of the universe, old age flowing free with the delicious near-by freedom of death.

Walt Whitman

When they came with the collection plate, they walked right past me like I was a penniless mugger.

Jimmy Savile, on attending Christmas Mass

The older we grow, the greater become the ordeals.

Johann Wolfgang von Goethe

A man over 90 is a great comfort to all his elderly neighbours: he is a picket-guard at the extreme outpost; and the young folks of 60 and 70 feel that the enemy must get by him before he can come near their camp.

Oliver Wendell Holmes

I've been grumpy since the age of 10, so it wasn't a generational shift.

I never expect anything to get better. I just am grumpy.

Sir Bob Geldof

I didn't turn into, at the age of 30, a grumpy old man, I was a grumpy teenager as well.

Rory McGrath

Every man desires to live long; but no man would be old.

Jonathan Swift

Men on Ageing

I think a lot about getting old. I don't want to be one of those 70-year-olds who still want lots of sex.

Rupert Everett

If we spent as much time feeling positive about getting older, as we do trying to stay young, how much different our lives would be.

Rob Brown

I think when the full horror of being 50 hits you; you should stay home and have a good cry.

Alan Bleasdale

Perhaps being old is having lighted rooms inside your head, and people in them, acting. People you know yet can't quite name.

Philip Larkin

I have found it to be true that the older I've become the better my life has become.

Rush Limbaugh

I think in 20 years I'll be looked at like Bob Hope. Doing those president jokes and golf sh*t. It scares me.

Eddie Murphy

At my age, I want to wake up and see sunshine pouring in through the windows every day.

John Cleese

Age is not a particularly interesting subject. Anyone can get old. All you have to do is live long enough.

Groucho Marx

Some mornings, it's just not worth chewing through the leather straps.

Emo Philips

As I get older I seem to believe less and less and yet to believe what I do believe more and more.

Gerald Brenan

You feel a little older in the morning. By noon I feel about 55.

Bob Dole

I still find each day too short for all the thoughts I want to think, all the walks I want to take, all the books I want to read, and all the friends I want to see.

John Burroughs

The more defects a man may have, the older he is, the less lovable, the more resounding his success.

Marquis de Sade

Few people know how to be old.

François de La Rochefoucauld

Men on Ageing

Most men do not mature, they simply grow taller.

Leo Rosten

I am my age. I'm not making any effort to change it.

Harrison Ford

The older I get, the more I become an apple pie, sparkling cider kind of guy.

Scott Foley

A man can be much amused when he hears himself seriously called an old man for the first time.

T. Kinnes

Age is how you feel. If you take care of yourself, you'll be able to do the same things. You may not do it as often. But you can still do it.

Barry Bonds

Nobody went out to pasture, and a lot of people are doing their best work. Bruce Springsteen, Tom Petty and Sting are at the top of their game. I mean, Tony Bennett is the coolest guy I ever met! We have to figure out how to break out of this age ghetto.

Bonnie Raitt

I know I can't cheat death, but I can cheat old age.

Darwin Deason

I like men who have a future and women who have a past.

Oscar Wilde

As one grows older one must try not to work oneself to death unnecessarily. At least that's how it is with me... I can scarcely keep pace and must watch out that the creative forces do not chase me around the universe in a wallop.

Carl Jung

Men of my age live in a state of continual desperation.

Trevor McDonald

Old age is an insult. It's like being smacked.

Lawrence Durrell

Old age: I fall asleep during the funerals of my friends.

Mason Cooley

I don't think I've gotten any smarter, but your reflexes slow down before you do something stupid when you're older.

Kris Kristofferson

I'm only two years older than Brad Pitt, but I look a lot older, which used to greatly frustrate me. It doesn't any more.

George Clooney

They're of a certain age, these ladies. You know, past their procreational best.

Ian McCaskill, discussing his admirers

Old age scares me. Almost everyone I know who is old is quite miserable, especially men.

Rupert Everett

Listen to Your Elders

Look to the future, because that is where you'll spend the rest of your life.

George Burns

Don't take life too seriously; you'll never get out of it alive.

Elbert Hubbard

You can add years to your life by wearing your pants backwards.

Johnny Carson

Don't smoke too much, drink too much, eat too much or work too much. We're all on the road to the grave – but there's no need to be in the passing lane.

Robert Orben

Stay humble. Always answer your phone – no matter who else is in the car.

Jack Lemmon

My mum died about three years ago at the age of 101, and just towards the end, as she began to run out of energy, she did actually stop trying to tell me what to do most of the time.

John Cleese

Forget past mistakes. Forget failures. Forget everything except what you are going to do now and do it.

William Durant

Do not do unto others as you expect they should do unto you; their tastes may not be the same.

George Bernard Shaw

First law on holes – when you're in one, stop digging.

Denis Healey

If at first you don't succeed, try, try again. Then quit. No use being a damn fool about it.

W.C. Fields

How people keep correcting us when we are young! There is always some bad habit or other they tell us we ought to get over. Yet most bad habits are tools to help us through life.

Jack Nicklaus

Listen to Your Elders

It is better to die on your feet than to live on your knees.

Dolores Ibarruri

The time to begin most things is 10 years ago.

Mignon McLaughlin

Never think you've seen the last of anything.

Eudora Welty

There are times not to flirt. When you're sick. When you're with children. When you're on the witness stand.

Joyce Jillson

Be bold. If you're going to make an error, make a doozey, and don't be afraid to hit the ball.

Billie Jean King

Find an aim in life before you run out of ammunition.

Arnold Glasow

I don't know the key to success, but the key to failure is trying to please everybody.

Bill Cosby

Always read stuff that will make you look good if you die in the middle of it.

P.J. O'Rourke

Never kick a fresh turd on a hot day.

Harry S. Truman

Be careful about reading health books. You might die of a misprint.

Mark Twain

Take the goods the gods provide, and don't stand and sulk when they are snatched away.

Mary McMullen

Go through your phone book, call people and ask them to drive you to the airport. The ones who will drive you are your true friends. The rest aren't bad people; they're just acquaintances.

Jay Leno

Be equal to your talent, not your age. At times let the gap between them be embarrassing.

Yevgeny Yevtushenko

At 46 one must be a miser; only have time for essentials.

Virginia Woolf

You can't have everything. Where would you put it?

Steven Wright

In real life, I assure you, there is no such thing as algebra.

Fran Lebowitz

Listen to Your Elders

Sometimes the road less travelled is less travelled for a reason.

Jerry Seinfeld

Never pick a fight with an ugly person, they've got nothing to lose.

Robin Williams

You can observe a lot just by watching.

Yogi Berra

There are only two ways of telling the complete truth – anonymously and posthumously.

Thomas Sowell

When you get to the end of your rope, tie a knot and hang on.

Franklin D. Roosevelt

Don't worry about the world coming to an end today. It's already tomorrow in Australia.

Charles M. Schulz

Be who you are and say what you feel, because those who mind don't matter and those who matter don't mind.

Dr. Seuss

You're only given a little spark of madness. You mustn't lose it.

Robin Williams

Son, always tell the truth. Then you'll never have to remember what you said the last time.

Sam Rayburn

Whatever you want to do, do it now. There are only so many tomorrows.

Michael Landon

Golden Oldies

FAMOUS OLDIES

I have enjoyed greatly the second blooming that comes when you finish the life of the emotions and of personal relations; and suddenly find – at the age of 50, say – that a whole new life has opened before you, filled with things you can think about, study, or read about… It is as if a fresh sap of ideas and thoughts was rising in you.

Agatha Christie

When you're a young man, Macbeth is a character part. When you're older, it's a straight part.

Laurence Olivier

Golden Oldies

Old age is like everything else. To make a success of it, you've got to start young.

Fred Astaire

I have the body of an 18-year-old. I keep it in the fridge.

Spike Milligan

One of the advantages of ageing is losing obsession about work and being able to spend some more time with your family.

Clint Eastwood

In his later years Pablo Picasso was not allowed to roam an art gallery unattended, for he had previously been discovered in the act of trying to improve on one of his old masterpieces.

Anon

You can't be as old as I am without waking up with a surprised look on your face every morning: 'Holy Christ, what da ya know – I'm still around!' It's absolutely amazing that I survived all the booze and smoking and the cars and the career.

Paul Newman

I used to desire many, many things, but now I have just one desire, and that's to get rid of all my other desires.

John Cleese

I shall not waste my days in trying to prolong them.

Ian L. Fleming

These days I am a teetotal, mean-spirited, right-wing, narrow-minded, conservative Christian bigot, but not a racist.

Jane Russell, speaking in 2003

I look forward to being older, when what you look like becomes less and less an issue and what you are is the point.

Susan Sarandon

Hollywood will accept actresses playing 10 years older, but actors can play 10 years younger.

Greta Scacchi

I have no regrets. I wouldn't have lived my life the way I did if I was going to worry about what people were going to say.

Ingrid Bergman

At my age I do what Mark Twain did. I get my daily paper, look at the obituaries page and if I'm not there I carry on as usual.

Patrick Moore

I feel like an old geezer!… Well, I am an old geezer.

Terry Wogan

Golden Oldies

I am affectionately known by Elton John as either Sylvia Disc or the Bionic Christian.

Sir Cliff Richard

In two years time I will be 50. But age doesn't hold any terrors for me because I feel stronger than ever.

Pierce Brosnan

I am not young enough to know everything.

Oscar Wilde

I will never give in to old age until I become old. And I'm not old yet!

Tina Turner

Getting old is a fascination thing. The older you get, the older you want to get.

Keith Richards

With 60 staring me in the face, I have developed inflammation of the sentence structure and a definite hardening of the paragraphs.

James Thurber

I love life because what more is there.

Anthony Hopkins

Golden Oldies

I am not the first man who wanted to make changes in his life at 60 and I won't be the last. It is just that others can do it with anonymity.

Harrison Ford

Everyone says I'm terrified of getting old but the truth is that in my job becoming old and extinct are one and the same thing.

Cher

My mother, God rest her soul, as soon as you gave her something, she would be eyeing it up to see who she could give it to when they turned up and she didn't have a present for them. You could see the virtual wrapping paper going around the thing you bought… you could see it was on its way to Doris next door.

Maureen Lipman, Grumpy Old Women

No sophisticated time schedule any more, that is something marvellous. Just cooking noodles, cultivating tomatoes, playing golf, lying in bed, eating chips with ketchup and spooning up peanut butter directly from the glass.

Celine Dion

I will actually say, 'Look, I'm very old and I'm very bored with you all, and I'm leaving.' It's one of the advantages of ageing – you can be eccentric and rude.

Sheila Hancock, Grumpy Old Women

Golden Oldies

Wouldn't it be great if people could get to live suddenly as often as they die suddenly?

Katharine Hepburn

Professionally, I have no age.

Kathleen Turner

I think I'm finally growing up – and about time.

Elizabeth Taylor

It is far better to be out with beautiful girls than be an old fart in the pub talking about what you were like in the 60s.

Mick Jagger

There are very little things in this life I cannot afford and patience is one of them.

Larry Hagman

Because young men are so goddamn disappointing!

Harrison Ford, explaining why women like older leading men

Things hurt me now. My knees hurt, my back hurts. But your head still thinks it's 23.

George Clooney

Harrison Ford may be getting old, but he can fight like a 28-year-old man.

Harrison Ford

Golfing Grandpas

If you watch a game, it's fun. If you play it, it's recreation. If you work at it, it's golf.

Bob Hope

Golf is a good walk spoiled.

Mark Twain

Golf is more fun than walking naked in a strange place, but not much.

Buddy Hackett

Playing golf is like going to a strip joint. After 18 holes you're tired and most of your balls are missing.

Tim Allen

The uglier a man's legs are, the better he plays golf – it's almost a law.

H. G. Wells

Golf is a fascinating game. It has taken me nearly 40 years to discover that I can't play it.

Ted Ray

When I die, bury me on the golf course so my husband will visit.

Anon

Golfing Grandpas

I would like to deny all allegations by Bob Hope that during my last game of golf, I hit an eagle, a birdie, an elk and a moose.

Gerald Ford

I'll shoot my age if I have to live to be 105.

Bob Hope

The only time my prayers are never answered is on the golf course.

Billy Graham

Sex and golf are the two things you can enjoy even if you're not good at them.

Kevin Costner

I know I'm getting better at golf because I'm hitting fewer spectators.

Gerald Ford

Eric: My wife says if I don't give up golf, she'll leave me.
Ernie: That's terrible.
Eric: I know – I'm really going to miss her.

Eric Morecombe and Ernie Wise

It was cool for a couple of weeks, but how much bad golf can you play?

John Goodman

Golfing Grandpas

It took me 17 years to get 3,000 hits in baseball. I did it in one afternoon on the golf course.

Hank Aaron

I had a wonderful experience on the golf course today. I had a hole in nothing. Missed the ball and sank the divot.

Don Adams

In the Bob Hope Golf Classic, the participation of President Gerald Ford was more than enough to remind you that the nuclear button was at one stage at the disposal of a man who might have either pressed it by mistake or else pressed it deliberately in order to obtain room service.

Clive James

The only way to enjoy golf is to be a masochist. Go out and beat yourself to death.

Howard Keel

If you think it's hard to meet new people, try picking up the wrong golf ball.

Jack Lemmon

If I wasn't an actor I'd be unemployable, or at best the secretary to a golf club somewhere. Nine holes at that, and blue in the face with port.

David Niven

Golfing Grandpas

I can't hit a ball more than 200 yards. I have no butt. You need a butt if you're going to hit a golf ball.

Dennis Quaid

I'm patient with crossword puzzles and the most impatient golfer.

Brett Hull

Golf is a day spent in a round of strenuous idleness.

William Wordsworth

I would rather play *Hamlet* with no rehearsal than TV golf.

Jack Lemmon

If you are caught on a golf course during a storm and are afraid of lightning, hold up a 1-iron. Not even God can hit a 1-iron.

Lee Trevino

Sport is a wonderful metaphor for life. Of all the sports that I played – skiing, baseball, fishing – there is no greater example than golf, because you're playing against yourself and nature.

Robert Redford

Golfing Grandpas

I don't have a life, I really don't. I'm as close to a nun as you can be without the little hat. I'm a golf nun.

Gabrielle Reece

In my retirement I go for a short swim at least once or twice every day. It's either that or buy a new golf ball.

Gene Perret

The reason the pro tells you to keep your head down is so you can't see him laughing.

Phyllis Diller

If you drink, don't drive. Don't even putt.

Dean Martin

If you are going to throw a club, it is important to throw it ahead of you, down the fairway, so you don't have to waste energy going back to pick it up.

Tommy Bolt

Acting has been good to me. It's taken me to play golf all over the world.

Christopher Lee

It is almost impossible to remember how tragic a place the world is when one is playing golf.

Robert Lynd

Long ago, when men cursed and beat the ground with sticks, it was called witchcraft. Today, it's called golf.

Anon

Golf: a game where white men can dress up as black pimps and get away with it.

Robin Williams

The golf course is the only place I can go dressed like a pimp and fit in perfectly. Anywhere else, lime-green pants and alligator shoes, I got a cop on my ass.

Samuel L. Jackson

I'm a coloured, one-eyed Jew… do I need anything else?

Sammy Davis Jr., in answer to a question:
What's your golf handicap?

The place of the father in the modern suburban family is a very small one, particularly if he plays golf.

Bertrand Russell

Geriatric Gardening

To get the best results you must talk to your vegetables.

Prince Charles

Geriatric Gardening

Though an old man, I am but a young gardener.

Thomas Jefferson

I want Death to find me planting my cabbages.

Michel De Montaigne

Planting is one of my great amusements, and even of those things which can only be for posterity, for a Septuagenary has no right to count on any thing but annuals.

Thomas Jefferson

If you want to be happy for a short time, get drunk; happy for a long time, fall in love; happy forever, take up gardening.

Arthur Smith

Live each day as if it were your last, and garden as though you will live forever.

Anon

What a man needs in gardening is a cast-iron back, with a hinge in it.

Charles Dudley Warner

In gardens, beauty is a by-product. The main business is sex and death.

Sam Llewellyn

Geriatric Gardening

Then again, if the plant is slow growing, and you are getting older, you may want to start with a larger plant. I find myself buying larger plants each year.

Bill Cannon

Cherry trees will blossom every year; but I'll disappear for good, one of these days.

Philip Whalen

We come from the earth, we return to the earth, and in between we garden.

Anon

Everything ends with flowers.

Hélène Cixous

If you are not killing plants, you are not really stretching yourself as a gardener.

J. C. Raulston

When gardening, I have one gift you won't find in any manuals. I know it's strange, but I can change perennials to annuals.

Dick Emmons

Old gardeners never die. They just spade away and then throw in the trowel.

Herbert V. Prochnow

I'm not ageing, I just need re-potting.

Anon

Now the gardener is the one who has seen
everything ruined so many times that (even as his
pain increases with each loss) he comprehends –
truly knows – that where there was a garden once,
it can be again, or where there never was, there yet
can be a garden.

Henry Mitchell

40 is about the age for unexpected developments:
extroverts turn introspective, introverts become
sociable, and everyone, without regard to type,
acquires grey hairs and philosophies of life. Many
also acquire gardens.

Janice Emily Bowens

Spicing up the Twilight Years

Once the travel bug bites there is no known
antidote, and I know that I shall be happily infected
until the end of my life.

Michael Palin

Football and cookery are the two most important
subjects in this country.

Delia Smith

Spicing up the Twilight Years

Life may not be the party we hoped for, but while we are here we might as well dance.

J. Williams

Give a man a fish and he has food for a day. Teach him how to fish and you can get rid of him for the entire weekend.

Zenna Schaffer

One of the worst things that can happen in life is to win a bet on a horse at an early age.

Danny McGoorty, Irish pool player

If people concentrated on the really important things in life, there'd be a shortage of fishing poles.

Doug Larson

There is a very fine line between 'hobby' and 'mental illness'.

Dave Barry

Hell, if I'd jumped on all the dames I'm supposed to have jumped on, I'd have had no time to go fishing.

Clark Gable

I go to Alaska and fish salmon. I do some halibut fishing, lake fishing, trout fishing, fly fishing. I look quite good in waders. I love my waders. I don't think there is anything sexier than just standing in waders with a fly rod. I just love it.

Linda Hamilton

I only make movies to finance my fishing.

Lee Marvin

Fishing is boring, unless you catch an actual fish, and then it is disgusting.

Dave Barry

I'm always suspicious of games where you're the only ones that play it.

Jack Charlton, on hurling

Skiing consists of wearing $3,000 worth of clothes and equipment and driving 200 miles in the snow in order to stand around at a bar and drink.

P. J. O'Rourke

There's a fine line between fishing and just standing on the shore like an idiot.

Steven Wright

Skiing combines outdoor fun with knocking down trees with your face.

Dave Barry

I'm Gonna Live Forever

The secret of longevity is to keep breathing.

Sophie Tucker

If man were immortal, do you realise what his meat bills would be?

Woody Allen

To lengthen thy life, lessen thy meals.

Benjamin Franklin

The secret to a long life is to stay busy, get plenty of exercise, and don't drink too much. Then again, don't drink too little.

Hermann Smith-Johansson, at age 103

Pretend to be dumb, that's the only way to reach old age.

Friedrich Dürrenmatt

A man 90 years old was asked to what he attributed his longevity.

'I reckon', he said, with a twinkle in his eye, 'it's because most nights I went to bed and slept when I should have sat up and worried.'

Dorothea Kent

I'm Gonna Live Forever

If you live to the age of a hundred you've made it because very few people die past the age of a hundred.

George Burns

My formula for living is quite simple. I get up in the morning and I go to bed at night. In between, I occupy myself as best I can.

Cary Grant

The only real way to look younger is not to be born so soon.

Charles M. Schulz

I've already lived about 20 years longer than my life expectancy at the time I was born. That's a source of annoyance to a great many people.

Ronald Reagan

I wanna live 'til I die, no more, no less.

Eddie Izzard

He had decided to live forever or die in the attempt.

Joseph Heller

Ageing seems to be the only available way to live a long life.

Daniel Auber

I'm Gonna Live Forever

Roz: Physical contact extends our lives.
Frasier: Well then, you'll outlive Styrofoam.

Frasier

There is a fountain of youth: it is your mind, your talents, the creativity you bring to your life and the lives of the people you love. When you learn to tap this source, you will truly have defeated age.

Sophia Loren

I postpone death by living, by suffering, by error, by risking, by giving, by losing.

Anais Nin

I am long on ideas, but short on time. I expect to live to be only about a hundred.

Thomas Alva Edison

We could certainly slow the ageing process down if it had to work its way through Congress.

Anon

My secret for staying young is good food, plenty of rest, and a make-up man with a spray gun.

Bob Hope

I'd like to grow very old as slowly as possible.

Irene Mayer Selznick

My only fear is that I may live too long. This would be a subject of dread to me.

Thomas Jefferson

I would not live forever, because we should not live forever, because if we were supposed to live forever, then we would live forever, but we cannot live forever, which is why I would not live forever.

Miss Alabama, 1994 Miss USA contest

Porridge is also the secret to a long life. I have it in the morning and it's the best start to the day.

Anon

Many Happy Returns

Most of us can remember a time when a birthday, especially if it was one's own, brightened the world as if a second sun had risen.

Robert Lynd

It is lovely, when I forget all birthdays, including my own, to find that somebody remembers me.

Ellen Glasgow

The formula for youth: Keep your enthusiasm and forget your birthdays.

Anon

Many Happy Returns

Don't send funny greeting cards on birthdays or at Christmas. Save them for funerals when their cheery effect is needed.

P.J. O'Rourke

What ought to be done to the man who invented the celebrating of anniversaries? Mere killing would be too light.

Mark Twain

I always add a year to myself, so I'm prepared for my next birthday. So when I was 39, I was already 40.

Nicolas Cage

When I was a kid I could toast marshmallows over my birthday candles. Now I could roast a turkey!

Anon

There comes a time when you should stop expecting other people to make a big deal about your birthday. That time is age 11.

Dave Barry

Is that a birthday? 'Tis, alas! too clear; 'tis but the funeral of the former year.

Alexander Pope

When a man has a birthday, he takes a day off.
When a woman has a birthday, she takes at least
three years off.

Joan Rivers

The best birthdays of all are those that haven't
arrived yet.

Robert Orben

From our birthday, until we die, is but the winking
of an eye.

William Butler Yeats

Last year my birthday cake looked like a prairie fire.
Rodney Dangerfield

You Can Teach an Old Dog New Tricks

When I was young I was amazed at Plutarch's
statement that the elder Cato began at the age of
80 to learn Greek. I am amazed no longer. Old age
is ready to undertake tasks that youth shirked
because they would take too long.

W. Somerset Maugham

Retirement is a Dirty Word

I enjoy going to the centre because I always get a lovely smile from the ladies there and I can impress them with new computer tips.

Lady, 100, attending computer classes

You are never too old. One of many examples, Grandma Moses (1860–1961), she started painting in her late 70s. She is best known for her documentary paintings of rural life. If you ever think you are too old, think of Grandma Moses!

Catherine Pulsifer

You are never too old to set another goal or to dream a new dream.

Les Brown

I'm having difficulty getting the doctors around here to sign the appropriate form.

Spike Milligan, on seeking permission to celebrate his eightieth birthday with a 12,000 foot skydive.

Retirement is a Dirty Word

Retirement at 65 is ridiculous. When I was 65 I still had pimples.

George Burns

Retirement is a Dirty Word

Never retire. Michelangelo was carving the *Rondanini* just before he died at 89. Verdi finished his opera *Falstaff* at 80. And the 80-year-old artist Goya scrawled on a drawing, 'I am still learning'.

Dr. W. Gifford-Jones

On announcing his retirement: You can only milk a cow for so long, then you're left holding the pail.

Hank Aaron

I'm mad, you know? I don't think of retiring at all.

Paul McCartney

People are always asking me when I'm going to retire. Why should I? I'm still making movies, and I'm a senior citizen, so I can see myself at half price.

George Burns

This is my final word. It is time for me to become an apprentice once more. I have not settled in which direction. But somewhere, sometime, soon.

Lord Beaverbrook, taken from his last public statement

Retirement is a Dirty Word

I don't want to retire. I'm not that good at crossword puzzles.

Norman Mailer

When old, retire from work, but not from life.

M.K. Soni

If youth is wasted on the young, then retirement is wasted on the old.

Anon

Retire? I'm going to stay in show business until I'm the only one left.

George Burns, age 90

At 85 you can only think ahead for the next 50 years or so.

Chuck Jones, on signing a long-term contract with Warner Brothers

Don't retire, retread!

Robert Otterbourg

Retirement is the period when you exchange the bills in your wallet for snapshots of your grandchildren.

Anon

Retirement is a Dirty Word

It's been different. I started driving again. I started cooking again. My driving's better than my cooking. George has discovered Sam's Club.

Barbara Bush

When a man retires and time is no longer a matter of urgent importance, his colleagues generally present him with a watch.

R.C. Sherriff

Retirement: That's when you return from work one day and say, 'Hi, honey, I'm home – forever.'

Gene Perret

You're 65 today – and it's the first day of the rest of your life savings.

Anon

Retirement? You're talking about death, right?

Robert Altman

Retirement kills more people than hard work ever did.

Malcolm Forbes

The trouble with retirement is that you never get a day off.

Abe Lemons

Retirement is a Dirty Word

I'm retired – goodbye tension, hello pension!

Anon

When a man retires, his wife gets twice the husband but only half the income.

Chi Chi Rodriguez

Retired is being twice tired, I've thought. First tired of working, then tired of not.

Richard Armour

Retirement: It's nice to get out of the rat race, but you have to learn to get along with less cheese.

Gene Perret

I love working. It's what I do best, and if I didn't work and tried to slow down, I'd just become a boring old fart.

Rik Mayall

Middle age is when work is a lot less fun and fun is a lot more work.

Anon

O, blest retirement! friend to life's decline –
How blest is he who crowns, in shades like these,
A youth of labour with an age of ease!

Oliver Goldsmith

Retirement is a Dirty Word

Retirement is wonderful. It's doing nothing without worrying about getting caught at it.

Gene Perret

There are some who start their retirement long before they stop working.

Robert Half

The question isn't at what age I want to retire, it's at what income.

George Foreman

The challenge of retirement is how to spend time without spending money.

Anon

Once it was impossible to find any Bond villains older than myself, I retired.

Roger Moore

Retirement means no pressure, no stress, no heartache… unless you play golf.

Gene Perret

Retirement must be wonderful. I mean, you can suck in your stomach for only so long.

Burt Reynolds

When you retire, think and act as if you were still working; when you're still working, think and act a bit as if you were already retired.

Anon

I've been trying for some time to develop a lifestyle that doesn't require my presence.

Gary Trudeau

Retirement – now life begins.

Catherine Pulsifer

Crowning Glory

By common consent, grey hairs are a crown of glory: the only object of respect that can never excite envy.

George Bancroft

There is only one cure for grey hair. It was invented by a Frenchman. It is called the guillotine.

P.G. Wodehouse

It is not by the grey of the hair that one knows the age of the heart.

Edward Bulwer-Lytton

Crowning Glory

It seems no more than right that men should seize time by the forelock, for the rude old fellow, sooner or later, pulls all their hair out.

George Dennison Prentice

There is more felicity on the far side of baldness than young men can possibly imagine.

Logan Pearsall Smith

Inflation is when you pay $15 for the $10 haircut you used to get for five dollars when you had hair.

Sam Ewing

Grey hair is God's graffiti.

Bill Cosby

I'm entering the 'metallic years'; silver in my hair, gold in my teeth and lead in my bottom!

Anon

André Gide was very bald with the general look of an elderly fallen angel travelling incognito.

Peter Quennell

On the bright side of life you will probably save a lot on shampoo when getting old and bald, and no longer have to suffer from thwarted and long gone ambitions.

T. Kinnes

Crowning Glory

After watching Cary Grant on a television broadcast, his mother, then in her 90s, reprimanded him for letting his hair get so grey. 'It doesn't bother me,' the actor replied carelessly. 'Maybe not,' said his mother, 'but it bothers *me*. It makes me seem so old.'

Anon

The best thing about being bald is when her folks come home; all you have to do is straighten your tie.

Milton Berle

He wore his baldness like an expensive hat.

Gloria Swanson

My husband was bending over to tie my three-year-old's shoes. That's when I noticed my son Ben staring at my husband's head. He gently touched the slightly thinning spot of hair and said in a concerned voice, 'Daddy, you have a hole in your head. Does it hurt?' After a pause, I heard my husband's murmured reply, 'Not physically.'

Reader's Digest

Women love a self-confident bald man.

Larry David

Crowning Glory

I'm not really bald. I just have a very wide parting.

Anon

The tenderest spot in a man's make-up is sometimes the bald spot on top of his head.

Helen Rowland

Violet will be a good colour for hair at just about the same time that brunette becomes a good colour for flowers.

Fran Lebowitz

The simple truth is that balding African-American men look cool when they shave their heads, whereas balding white men look like giant thumbs.

Dave Barry

Grey hairs are signs of wisdom if you hold your tongue. Speak and they are but hairs, as in the young.

Anon

We're all born bald, baby.

Telly Savalas

I feel old when I see mousse in my opponent's hair.

Andre Agassi

Crowning Glory

I'm not bald… I'm just taller than my hair.

Clive Anderson

I know body hair bothers some women, but a lot of men like a fluffy partner.

Dame Edna Everage

You can always tell where Diana Ross has been by the hair that's left behind!

Diana Ross

The secret of my success is my hairspray.

Richard Gere

A man is usually bald four or five years before he knows it.

Ed Howe

The worst thing a man can do is go bald. Never let yourself go bald.

Donald Trump

He's the kind of guy that when he dies, he's going up to heaven and give God a bad time for making him bald.

Marlon Brando, on Frank Sinatra

It's a question that I find like asking somebody, 'Did you have a breast implant?' or 'When did you get your lobotomy?

William Shatner, when asked if he wore a hairpiece

My hairdresser actually spends more time digging hair out of my ears than off the top or back of my head.

Des Lynam, Grumpy Old Men

When others kid me about being bald, I simply tell them that the way I figure it, the good Lord only gave men so many hormones, and if others want to waste theirs on growing hair, that's up to them.

John Glenn

A hair in the head is worth two in the brush.

Don Herold

Teething Troubles

I had very good dentures once. Some magnificent gold work. It's the only form of jewellery a man can wear that women fully appreciate.

Graham Greene

Dentures: Two rows of artificial ivories that may be removed periodically to frighten one's grandchildren or provide accompaniment to Spanish music.

Anon

It is after you have lost your teeth that you can afford to buy steaks.

Pierre Auguste Renoir

Teething Troubles

We idolised the Beatles, except for those of us who idolised the Rolling Stones, who in those days still had many of their original teeth.

Dave Barry

I've gotten to the age where I need my false teeth and hearing aid before I can ask where I left my glasses.

Anon

I don't have false teeth. Do you think I'd buy teeth like these?

Carol Burnett

Every tooth in a man's head is more valuable than a diamond.

Miguel de Cervantes

I like my bifocals,
my dentures fit me fine,
my hearing aid is perfect,
but Lord I miss my mind!

Anon

She had so many gold teeth… she used to have to sleep with her head in a safe.

W.C. Fields

Now Bart, since you broke Grandpa's teeth, he gets to break yours.

Homer Simpson, The Simpsons

The good news about mid-life is that the glass is still half-full. Of course, the bad news is that it won't be long before your teeth are floating in it.

Anon

Ribs, great… why don't you just kick the dentures out of my mouth?

Sophia Petrillo, The Golden Girls

I swear if Colgate comes out with one more type of toothpaste. I just want clean teeth; that's all I want. I don't want the tartar and I don't want the cavities. And I want white teeth. How come I have to choose? And then they have the 'Colgate Total' that supposedly has everything in there. I don't believe that for one second. If it's all in the one, how come they make all the others? Who's going: 'I don't mind the tartar so much'?

Ellen DeGeneres

God gives nuts to those with no teeth.

Anon

I Shall Wear Purple

After 50 a man discovers he does not need more than one suit.

Clifton Fadiman

Being home on a Friday night with the old man, an Indian take-away and a nice bottle of wine, and there's something on the telly, oh, I like that. I'm in my dressing gown, I mean it's not a weird dressing gown, it's not one of those quilted old lady ones. It's Cath Kidston. It's quite a funky dressing gown… don't get me wrong. I'm not that old.

Jenny Eclair, Grumpy Old Women

If women dressed for men, the stores wouldn't sell much – just an occasional sun visor.

Groucho Marx

Underwear makes me uncomfortable and besides my parts have to breathe.

Jean Harlow

Trying on pants is one of the most humiliating things a man can suffer that doesn't involve a woman.

Larry David

You'd be surprised how much it costs to look this cheap.

Dolly Parton

I Shall Wear Purple

I am 56 years old, an age when many women tend not to be noticed as we plod about in our extra wide, midi-heeled sensible shoes.

Sue Townsend

You can say what you like about long dresses, but they cover a multitude of shins.

Mae West

She looked as if she had been poured into her clothes and had forgotten to say 'when'.

P. G. Wodehouse

Brevity is the soul of lingerie.

Dorothy Parker

Dress simply. If you wear a dinner jacket, don't wear anything else on it… like lunch or dinner.

George Burns

Nothing goes out of fashion sooner than a long dress with a very low neck.

Coco Chanel

Fashion is what you adopt when you don't know who you are.

Quentin Crisp

I Shall Wear Purple

The only man I know who behaves sensibly is my tailor; he takes my measurements anew each time he sees me. The rest go on with their old measurements and expect me to fit them.

George Bernard Shaw

If God had meant us to walk around naked, he would never have invented the wicker chair.

Erma Bombeck

Gloves complete a look. That's my belief. Who cares if I'm right or wrong? I had a mother who encouraged me to go with impulses. And I have, and it's led to some insanely ridiculous outfits, but I like it that way.

Diane Keaton

I wouldn't say I invented tacky, but I definitely brought it to its present high popularity.

Bette Midler

How on earth did Gandhi manage to walk so far in flip-flops? I can't last 10 minutes in mine.

Mrs. Merton

I don't think I would've worn thongs even when I was young and trying very hard. No, that's ridiculous. You might as well go without knickers at all.

Annette Crosbie, Grumpy Old Women

I Shall Wear Purple

And you know, the baby boomers are getting older, and those off the rack clothes are just not fitting right any longer, and so, tailor-made suits are coming back into fashion.

Amy Irving

I base my fashion taste on what doesn't itch.

Gilda Radner

Now that I'm old [clothes shopping] has become entirely frustrating because there is nothing for me to wear in the shops. Nothing. I mean, I'm not going to wear hipster pants, am I? If I wear hipster pants and I sit down, I'll shoot out the back of them. It's not on.

Germaine Greer, Grumpy Old Women

Show me a man with both feet on the ground and I'll show you a man who can't get his pants on.

Joe E. Lewis

Tell me the history of that frock, Janet. It's obviously an old favourite. You were wise to remove the curtain rings. I love that fabric. You were lucky to find so much of it.

Dame Edna Everage

I Shall Wear Purple

Once you can accept the universe as matter expanding into nothing that is something, wearing stripes with plaid comes easy.

Albert Einstein

Women's clothes: never wear anything that panics the cat.

P.J. O'Rourke

Some women hold up dresses that are so ugly and they always say the same thing: 'This looks much better on.' On what? On fire?

Marsha Warfield

Hilary: One of the few lessons I have learned in life is that there is invariably something odd about women who wear ankle socks.

Alan Bennett, The Old Country

Fashion is a form of ugliness so intolerable that we have to alter it every six months.

Oscar Wilde

I grow old… I grow old… I shall wear the bottoms of my trousers rolled.

T.S. Eliot

I wouldn't say her bathing suit was skimpy, but I've seen more cotton in the top of an aspirin bottle.

Henny Youngman

Denise: Dad, stop fiddling with yerself.
Jim: I'm not fiddling with meself. I paid a quid for these underpants and I've got 50 pence stuck up me arse.

Denise and Jim Royle, The Royle Family

I know what Victoria's Secret is. The secret is that nobody older than 30 can fit into their stuff.

Sima Jacobson

A hat should be taken off when you greet a lady and left off for the rest of your life. Nothing looks more stupid than a hat.

P.J. O'Rourke

Though I am grateful for the blessings of wealth, it hasn't changed who I am. My feet are still on the ground. I'm just wearing better shoes.

Oprah Winfrey

I never cared for fashion much, amusing little seams and witty little pleats: it was the girls I liked.

David Bailey

Young at Heart

He says he feels young at heart but slightly older in other places.

Anon

Young at Heart

Another belief of mine: that everyone else my age is an adult, whereas I am merely in disguise.

Margaret Atwood

You can't help getting older, but you don't have to get old.

George Burns

You're only young once, but you can be immature forever.

John Greier

One starts to get young at the age of 60 and then it is too late.

Pablo Picasso

When I was 10, I read fairy tales in secret and would have been ashamed if I had been found doing so. Now that I am 50, I read them openly. When I became a man, I put away childish things – including the fear of childishness and the desire to be grown-up.

C.S. Lewis

Setting a good example for your children takes all the fun out of middle age.

William Feather

I have spent my whole life – up to a minute ago – being younger than I am now.

John Ciardi

Except for an occasional heart attack I feel as young as I ever did.

Robert Benchley

Try to keep your soul young and quivering right up to old age.

George Sand

Life would be infinitely happier if we could only be born at the age of 80 and gradually approach 18.

Mark Twain

Over the Hill

I'm so old they've cancelled my blood type.

Bob Hope

I'd rather be over the hill than under it.

Anon

To live beyond 80 is an exaggeration, almost an excess.

Antonio Callado

Over the Hill

Wrecked on the lee shore of age.

Sarah Orne Jewett

Just remember, once you're over the hill you begin to pick up speed.

Charles M. Schulz

You know you're over the hill when the only whistles you get are from the tea kettle.

Anon

The follies which a man regrets most in his life are those which he didn't commit when he had the opportunity.

Helen Rowland

I didn't get old on purpose, it just happened. If you're lucky it could happen to you.

Andy Rooney

A lot of people start to fall to bits at 30… quite honestly once you are able to reproduce you're over the hill. You start to go downhill at 18 physically.

Mick Jagger

Over the hill? I don't remember any hill?!

Anon

I'm too beat-up and old now to be a sex symbol.

Mel Gibson

I've been around so long I can remember Doris Day before she was a virgin.

Groucho Marx

I'm too old for this sh★t!

Danny Glover, as Roger Murtaugh, Lethal Weapon

You're not over the hill until you hear your favourite songs in an elevator!

Anon

My veins are filled once a week with a Neapolitan carpet cleaner distilled from the Adriatic and I am as bald as an egg. However, I still get around and am mean to cats.

John Cheever

I'd Rather Have a Cup of Tea

Growing old is when you resent the swimsuit issue of *Sports Illustrated* because there are fewer articles to read.

George Burns

I'd Rather Have a Cup of Tea

Everyone probably thinks that I'm a raving nymphomaniac, that I have an insatiable sexual appetite, when the truth is I'd rather read a book.

Madonna

Middle age is having a choice of two temptations and choosing the one that will get you home earlier.

Dan Bennett

Now that I think of it, I wish I had been a hell-raiser when I was 30 years old. I tried it when I was 50 but I always got sleepy.

Groucho Marx

My wife is a sex object. Every time I ask for sex, she objects.

Les Dawson

I only watch *Baywatch* for the articles.

Chief Dan

They say marriages are made in Heaven. But so is thunder and lightning.

Clint Eastwood

I don't want to snog old men, with their yellow horrible teeth, old crinkly skin and hairy moles.

Cilla Black

I'd Rather Have a Cup of Tea

Thank God! Now I realise I've been chained to an idiot for the last 60 years of my life!

Kingsley Amis at 70, on his lost libido

The important thing in acting is to be able to laugh and cry. If I have to cry, I think of my sex life. If I have to laugh, I think of my sex life.

Glenda Jackson

I haven't had sex in eight months. To be honest, I now prefer to go bowling.

Anon

As I get older, I just prefer to knit.

Tracey Ullman

I'm at the age where I want two girls. In case I fall asleep they will have someone to talk to.

Rodney Dangerfield

Sex is a bad thing because it rumples the clothes.

Jackie Onassis

I am happy now that Charles calls on my bedchamber less frequently than of old. As it is, I now endure but two calls a week and when I hear his steps outside my door I lie down on my bed, close my eyes, open my legs and think of England.

Lady Alice Hillingdon

All this fuss about sleeping together. For physical pleasure I'd sooner go to my dentist any day.

Evelyn Waugh

My wife only has sex with me for a purpose. Last night it was to time an egg.

Rodney Dangerfield

Forever Young

I believe in loyalty. When a woman reaches a certain age she likes, she should stick with it.

Eva Gabor

The trick is growing up without growing old.

Casey Stengel

I was wise enough to never grow up while fooling most people into believing I had.

Margaret Mead

The best thing about growing older is that it takes such a long time.

Anon

She was a handsome woman of 45 and would remain so for many years.

Anita Brookner

Forever Young

To win back my youth... there is nothing I wouldn't do – except take exercise, get up early, or be a useful member of the community.

Oscar Wilde

By the time I'd grown up, I naturally supposed that I'd grown up.

Eve Babitz

Being loved keeps you young.

Madonna

I'm saving that rocker for the day when I feel as old as I really am.

Dwight D. Eisenhower

I'm not denying my age, I'm embellishing my youth.

Tamara Reynolds

In an ideal world I would like to be alive until I am dead.

Sir John Harvey-Jones

Cheerfulness and contentment are great beautifiers, and are famous preservers of youthful looks.

Charles Dickens

Pushing 40? She's hanging on for dear life.

Ivy Compton-Burnett

She has discovered the secret of perpetual middle age.

Oscar Levant

The Pipe and Slipper Brigade

SMOKING

But when I don't smoke I scarcely feel as if I'm living. I don't feel as if I'm living unless I'm killing myself.

Russell Hoban

I have every sympathy with the American who was so horrified by what he had read of the effects of smoking that he gave up reading.

Henry G. Strauss

I would reintroduce smoking everywhere.

Martin Burton, head of Zippo's Circus, tells *Time Out* magazine how he would tackle being Mayor of London

I don't smoke, but I'd rather be with my pals who do than sitting alone in a pub with no people and no atmosphere.

Brian Monteith, Conservative MSP for
Mid–Scotland and Fife

The Pipe and Slipper Brigade

At least by going to the jungle I won't have people telling me where and when I can smoke. Wish me luck and keep on smoking, if you want to.

Antony Worrall Thompson

My inspiration has always been Jeanne Calment, a Frenchwoman who smoked and drank every day and died a few years ago at the age of 122. When asked the secret of her longevity, she replied: 'I laugh a lot.' Well, you would, wouldn't you?

Victoria Coren

My doctor phoned and said you don't deserve this news, but your lungs are crystal clear.

Chainsmoker Nicky Haslam, at age 63

Smokers of the world unite! We have been bullied and nannied long enough. And if Tony Blair is tempted to follow the lead of Ireland and Italy, let us remind him that only 10.7 million voted Labour last time. But 15 million smoke.

Tom Utley

Smokers pay £19,000 a minute to the Exchequer, and that's enough to pay for the whole police force. Or to put it another way, for every £1 we cost the NHS, we give it £3.60. Please don't encourage the state to dictate how I live my life.

Jeremy Clarkson

The Pipe and Slipper Brigade

I never allow myself to be photographed if I'm not smoking. It's a strict policy I've adhered to for a long time. I initiated it when it became politically correct not to smoke.

Maggi Hambling, on being photographed
without a cigarette

I know Fabien [Barthez] smokes… In England, it's a rare thing to see a player smoking but, all in all, I prefer that to an alcoholic.

Sir Alex Ferguson

When I smoked myself – up to 60 on some working days – I resolved never to become an anti-smoking bore because I hated them so much. By and large I've stuck to that: if people ask to smoke in our house we gladly cry, 'Yes, of course! Here are ashtrays, cigar clippers, pipe reamers, hookahs, oxygen masks – anything you need!'

Simon Hoggart

Apparently cigarettes contain embalming fluid. This explains why I'm possibly the best-preserved woman in Britain.

Sue Carroll

Smoking, I would now suggest, may be here to stay.

James Walton, editor of The Faber Book of Smoking

The Pipe and Slipper Brigade

I used to smoke all the time but four years ago I changed my smoking habit to smoke only when I'm drinking. However, this policy has had an adverse effect on my drinking habits.

Tommy Walsh

I might smoke more.

Jeremy Irons, announcing his New Year resolution

I enjoy it too much.

David Bowie, explaining why he will never give up smoking

If you want to smoke you should be allowed to do so. For those who smoke it is a natural, relaxing part of life.

Antony Worrall Thompson

When on occasion I'm asked by groups of aspiring writers what they should do to get on, my advice is always, emphatically, smoke. Smoke often and smoke with gusto. It's a little known, indeed little researched, fact of literature and journalism that no non-smoker is worth reading. And writers who give up become crashing bores.

A.A. Gill

The Pipe and Slipper Brigade

Oh, I like smoking, I do. I smoke for my health, my mental health. Tobacco gives you little pauses, a rest from life. I don't suppose anyone smoking a pipe would have road rage, would they?

David Hockney

If I'm seen smoking in the street, people should come up to me and say thank you very much for keeping my tax bill down.

Jeremy Clarkson

I neither coughed nor felt sick. Instead, a sensation of wellbeing filled me, and I became slightly wired, not the reaction you get from alcohol, but sharper and calmer.

John Simpson, experiencing a cigar for the first time

Smoking is, if not my life, then at least my hobby. I love to smoke. Smoking is fun. Smoking is cool. Smoking is, as far as I'm concerned, the entire point of being an adult.

Fran Lebowitz

And a woman is only a woman, but a good cigar is a smoke.

Rudyard Kipling, The Betrothed

It is now proven, beyond a doubt, that smoking is a leading cause of statistics.

Fletcher Knebel

The Pipe and Slipper Brigade

If I cannot smoke in heaven, then I shall not go.

Mark Twain

I want all hellions to quit puffing that hell fume in God's clean air.

Carry Nation

Having smoking and non-smoking sections in the same room is like having urinating and non-urinating sections in a swimming pool.

Ross Parker

I finally quit smoking by using the patch. I put six of them over my mouth.

Wendy Liebman

Giving up smoking is the easiest thing in the world. I know because I've done it thousands of times.

Mark Twain

They say if you smoke you knock off 10 years. But it's the last 10. What do you miss? The drooling years?

John Mendoza

I've been smoking for 30 years now and there's nothing wrong with my lung.

Freddie Starr

Smoking is very bad for you and should only be done because it looks so good. People who don't smoke have a terrible time finding something polite to do with their lips.

P.J. O'Rourke

Pass the Port

DRINK

I have been advised by the best medical authority, at my age, not to attempt to give up alcohol.

W.C. Fields

I love everything that's old – old friends, old times, old manners, old books, old wine.

Oliver Goldsmith, She Stoops to Conquer

I've stopped drinking, but only while I'm asleep.

George Best

A man is a fool if he drinks before he reaches the age of 50, and a fool if he doesn't afterward.

Frank Lloyd Wright

Actually, it only takes one drink to get me loaded. Trouble is, I can't remember if it's the thirteenth or fourteenth.

George Burns

The problem with the world is that everyone is a few drinks behind.

Humphrey Bogart

I exercise strong self-control. I never drink anything stronger than gin before breakfast.

W.C. Fields

You're not drunk if you can lie on the floor without holding on.

Joe E. Lewis

I was in for 10 hours and had 40 pints – beating my previous record by 20 minutes.

George Best, on a blood transfusion for his liver transplant, not on his drinking

Always do sober what you said you'd do drunk. That will teach you to keep your mouth shut.

Ernest Hemingway

Beer is proof that God loves us and wants us to be happy.

Benjamin Franklin

I'm not a heavy drinker; I can sometimes go for hours without touching a drop.

Noel Coward

Pass the Port

An alcoholic is anyone you don't like who drinks more than you do.

Dylan Thomas

I know I'm drinking myself to a slow death, but then I'm in no hurry.

Robert Benchley

I often sit back and think, I wish I'd done that and find out later that I already have.

Richard Harris, describing the effects of drinking

I am a drinker with writing problems.

Brendan Behan

I feel sorry for people who don't drink. They wake up in the morning and that's the best they're going to feel all day.

Dean Martin

The difference between a drunk and an alcoholic is that a drunk doesn't have to attend all those meetings.

Arthur Lewis

A tavern is a place where madness is sold by the bottle.

Jonathan Swift

One more drink and I'll be under the host.

Dorothy Parker

The problem with some people is that when they aren't drunk, they're sober.

William Butler Yeats

Beer commercials are so patriotic: 'Made the American Way.' What does that have to do with America? Is that what America stands for? Feeling sluggish and urinating frequently?

Evelyn Waugh

A woman drove me to drink and I didn't even have the decency to thank her.

W.C. Fields

Sometimes when I reflect back on all the beer I drink I feel ashamed. Then I look into the glass and think about the workers in the brewery and all of their hopes and dreams. If I didn't drink this beer, they might be out of work and their dreams would be shattered. Then I say to myself, 'It is better that I drink this beer and let their dreams come true than to be selfish and worry about my liver.'

Jack Handey

I saw a notice that said 'Drink Canada Dry' and I've just started.

Brendan Behan

Pass the Port

I formed a new group called Alcoholics Unanimous. If you don't feel like a drink, you ring another member and he comes over to persuade you.

Richard Harris

Good old days: Beer foamed and drinking water didn't.

Anon

Be wary of strong drink. It can make you shoot at tax collectors... and miss.

Robert A. Heinlein

Milk is for babies. When you grow up you have to drink beer.

Arnold Schwarzenegger

Beer, it's the best damn drink in the world.

Jack Nicholson

I drink too much. The last time I gave a urine sample it had an olive in it.

Rodney Dangerfield

I believe all drunks go to heaven, because they've been through hell on Earth.

Liza Minnelli

When I was a practising alcoholic, I was unbelievable. One side effect was immense suspicion: I'd come off tour like Inspector Clouseau on acid. 'Where's this cornflake come from? It wasn't here before.'

Ozzy Osbourne

When I read about the evils of drinking, I gave up reading.

Henny Youngman

I have a rare intolerance to herbs, which means I can only drink fermented liquids, such as gin.

Julie Walters

Fading Away

MEMORY LOSS

As you get older three things happen. The first is your memory goes, and I can't remember the other two.

Sir Norman Wisdom

I believe the true function of age is memory. I'm recording as fast as I can.

Rita Mae Brown

Fading Away

Just sometimes you bump into people and you think, 'You're my best friend, aren't you? I recognise you. Ooh, you're looking old. What's your name?'

Jenny Eclair, Grumpy Old Women

It's hard to be nostalgic when you can't remember anything.

Anon

Did you ever walk in a room and forget why you walked in? I think that's how dogs spend their lives.

Sue Murphy

Maturity is different from using your ailing health to blackmail your children into doing all your gardening and housework and keeping a diary for comfort and a handy reminder of what you did yesterday.

T. Kinnes

Women over 50 don't have babies because they would put them down and forget where they left them.

Anon

Isn't this amazing? Clinton is getting $8 million for his memoir, Hillary got $8 million for her memoir. That is $16 million for two people who for eight years couldn't remember anything.

Jay Leno

My memory is going. I brush my teeth, and then 10 minutes later I go back and have to feel the toothbrush. Is it wet? Did I just brush them?

Terry Gilliam

I'm suffering from Mallzheimer's disease. I go to the mall and forget where I parked my car.

Anon

I think it would be interesting if old people got anti-Alzheimer's disease where they slowly began to recover other people's lost memories.

George Carlin

Senior Moments

For those of you haven't read the book, it's being published tomorrow.

David Frost

And there's the Victoria Memorial, built as a memorial to Victoria.

David Dimbleby

Richard Burton had a tremendous passion for the English language, especially the spoken and written word.

Frank Bough

Senior Moments

It will take time to restore chaos and order.

George W. Bush

Beginning in February 1976 your assistance benefits will be discontinued… Reason: it has been reported to our office that you expired on January 1, 1976.

Excerpt from a letter, Illinois Department of Public Aid

My shoes are size two and a half, the same size as my feet.

Elaine Page

I didn't know *Onward Christian Soldiers* was a Christian song.

Aggie Pate, at a non-denominational mayor's breakfast, Fort Worth, Texas

The Holocaust was an obscene period in our nation's history… this century's history… We all lived in this century. I didn't live in this century.

Dan Quayle

Was it you or your brother who was killed in the war?

Rev. William Spooner

Fiction writing is great. You can make up almost anything.

Ivana Trump, upon finishing her first novel

A bachelor's life is no life for a single man.

Samuel Goldwyn

I love California; I practically grew up in Phoenix.

Dan Quayle

You seem to be a man who likes to keep his feet on the ground – you sail a lot.

Alan Titchmarsh

The Rolling Stones suffered a great loss with the death of Ian Stewart, the man who had for so many years played piano quietly and silently with them on stage.

Andy Peebles

Elderly American lady: 'You speak very good English.'
Me: 'Thank you, but that's because I come from the United Kingdom.'
Elderly American lady: 'Oh, I didn't know they teach English over there.'

Anon

Republicans understand the importance of bondage between a mother and child.

Dan Quayle

Cardial – as in cardial arrest.

Eve Pollard

Your ambition – is that right – is to abseil across the English Channel?

Cilla Black

I haven't read any of the autobiographies about me.

Elizabeth Taylor

The nice thing about being senile is you can hide your own Easter eggs.

Anon

To see what is in front of one's nose needs a constant struggle.

George Orwell

I never know how much of what I say is true.

Bette Midler

The future ain't what it used to be.

Yogi Berra

I am wonderful, with a perfect physique, very charming, rich and look like Jude Law.

Peter Stringfellow

I've always thought that underpopulated countries in Africa are vastly underpolluted.

> *Lawrence Summers,* chief economist of the World Bank

He hits from both sides of the plate. He's amphibious.

> *Yogi Berra*

One year ago today, the time for excuse-making has come to an end.

> *George W. Bush*

It's always been my dream to come to Madison Square Garden and be the warm-up act for Elvis.

> *Al Gore*

Outside of the killings, Washington has one of the lowest crime rates in the country.

> *Mayor Marion Barry,* Washington, D.C.

I haven't committed a crime. What I did was fail to comply with the law.

> *David Dinkins,* New York City Mayor

And so, in my State of the – my State of the Union – or state – my speech to the nation, whatever you want to call it, speech to the nation – I asked Americans to give 4,000 years – 4,000 hours over the next – the rest of your life – of service to America. That's what I asked – 4,000 hours.

George W. Bush

Abortion is advocated only by persons who have themselves been born.

Ronald Reagan

Driving Miss Daisy

I suppose when I am driving, particularly in London, the thing that makes me angriest is cyclists, the anarchists of the road… they weave in and out, ignore the traffic lights and then if you dare go anywhere near them, they scream at you like banshees. There's this extraordinary assumption that we will all have to get out of their way. But they can do what they damn well like.

Sheila Hancock, Grumpy Old Women

Regular naps prevent old age, especially if you take them while driving.

Anon

When I am in the car I can have a nice scream because I am contained. I scream very, very loudly, or I scream filthy words and nasty expletives, and nobody can hear.

Michele Hanson, Grumpy Old Women

Have you ever noticed that anybody driving slower than you is an idiot, and anyone going faster than you is a maniac?

George Carlin

If I stop at a zebra crossing, I stop and wave and I'd like them to wave. But if they don't, then I think, 'Well, you bastard, this is the last time I'm gonna do this for you'.

Don Warrington, Grumpy Old Men

Never drive faster than your Guardian Angel can fly.

Anon

Driving Miss Daisy

Apparently more than 80 per cent of open-top sports cars are sold to sad sacks who believe this throbbing mechanical extension makes them look young and virile, not old and desperate.

Amanda Craig

Driving is a spectacular form of amnesia. Everything is to be discovered, everything to be obliterated.

Jean Baudrillard

Drive carefully! Remember, it's not only a car that can be recalled by its maker.

Anon

I drive with my knees. Otherwise, how can I put on my lipstick and talk on my phone?

Sharon Stone

The worst drivers are women in people carriers, men in white vans and anyone in a baseball cap. That's just about everyone.

Paul O'Grady

You know, somebody actually complimented me on my driving today. They left a little note on the windscreen; it said 'Parking Fine.'

Tommy Cooper

Driving Miss Daisy

As a senior citizen was driving down the freeway, his car phone rang. Answering, he heard his wife's voice urgently warning him, 'Henry, I just heard on the news that there's a car going the wrong way on 280. Please be careful!' Henry said, 'Hell, it's not just one car. It's hundreds of them!'

Anon

I hate driving more than anything in the whole world. I'm just an awful, awful driver. I get lost, I hit things: parked cars, one moving car, a pole in my parking garage. Just when I think I got everything under control, I'll miss seeing something out of the corner of my mirror.

Rachel Leigh

Sure, I've gotten old. I've had two bypass surgeries, a hip replacement, new knees… I've fought prostate cancer and diabetes. I'm half blind, can't hear anything quieter than a jet engine, and take 40 different medications that make me dizzy, winded and subject to blackouts. I have bouts with dementia, poor circulation, hardly feel my hands or feet any more, can't remember if I'm 85 or 92, but… thank God, I still have my Florida driver's licence.

Anon

The best car safety device is a rear-view mirror with a cop in it.

Dudley Moore

If you stay in Beverly Hills too long you become a Mercedes.

Robert Redford

Pounds, shillings and pence

Money isn't everything, but it sure keeps you in touch with your children.

J. Paul Getty

I've got all the money I'll ever need if I die by four o'clock this afternoon.

Henny Youngman

Money is something you have to make in case you don't die.

Max Asnas

I'm living so far beyond my income that we may almost be said to be living apart.

e.e. cummings

There's no reason to be the richest man in the cemetery. You can't do any business from there.

Colonel Sanders

Another good thing about being poor is that when you are 70 your children will not have declared you legally insane in order to gain control of your estate.

Woody Allen

Most men love money and security more, and creation and construction less, as they get older.

John Maynard Keynes

Parents should be given only a modest and sensible allowance. And they should be encouraged to save up for things. This builds character. It also helps pay for the funeral.

P.J. O'Rourke

Vintage Vigour

I don't exercise. If God wanted me to bend over, he'd have put diamonds on the floor.

Joan Rivers

I get my exercise running to the funerals of my friends who exercise.

Barry Gray

I consider exercise vulgar. It makes people smell.

Alec Yuill Thornton

Vintage Vigour

To resist the frigidity of old age, one must combine the body, the mind, and the heart. And to keep these in parallel vigour one must exercise, study, and love.

Alan Bleasdale

Once I realised how expensive funerals are, I began to exercise and watch my diet.

Thomas Sowell

If God wanted me to touch my toes, he would have put them on my knees.

Roseanne Barr

I get my exercise acting as a pallbearer to my friends who exercise.

Chauncey Depew

Exercise is bunk. If you are healthy you don't need it. If you are sick you shouldn't take it.

Henry Ford

I like long walks, especially when they are taken by people who annoy me.

Fred Allen

My idea of exercise is a good brisk sit down.

Phyllis Diller

Jogging is very beneficial. It's good for your legs and your feet. It's also very good for the ground. It makes it feel needed.

Charles M. Schulz

Jogging is for people who aren't intelligent enough to watch television.

Victoria Wood

In the gym, I only wear black and diamonds.

Donatella Versace

You know you're into middle age when first you realise that caution is the only thing you care to exercise.

Charles Ghigna

The trouble with jogging is that by the time you realise you're not in shape for it, it's too far to walk back.

Franklin P. Jones

I often take exercise. Only yesterday I had breakfast in bed.

Oscar Wilde

I bought all those celebrity exercise videos. I love to sit and eat cookies and watch them.

Dolly Parton

Vintage Vigour

I have a punishing workout regimen. Every day I do three minutes on a treadmill, then I lie down, drink a glass of vodka and smoke a cigarette.

Anthony Hopkins

I've exercised with women so thin that buzzards followed them to their cars.

Erma Bombeck

I diet every day of my life. After 40 you've got to.

Kim Cattrall

Passing the vodka bottle. And playing the guitar.

Keith Richards, on how he keeps fit

I do try and keep fit, but it's a half-hearted battle. I'll go for a jog once a fortnight and then feel ill for two days afterwards. And now and again I'll join a health club, but the trauma of filling in the form and having my photo taken for the membership card usually puts me off going for about 12 months. But I'm still optimistic that one day I'll be offered a guest role in *Baywatch*.

Steve Coogan

The first time I see a jogger smiling, I'll consider it.

Joan Rivers

Sometimes I run around Regent's Park and go to the gym, I can manage about an hour, but stop for a cigarette every so often.

Julian Clary

You know you've reached middle age when your weightlifting consists of merely standing up.

Bob Hope

A Quiet Five Minutes

THE AFTERNOON NAP

I'll sleep when I'm dead.

Warren Zevon

Sleep – those little slices of death, how I loathe them.

Edgar Allan Poe

No day is so bad it can't be fixed with a nap.

Carrie Snow

Two things I dislike about my granddaughter – when she won't take her afternoon nap, and when she won't let me take mine.

Gene Perret

I usually take a two-hour nap from one to four.

Yogi Berra

A Quiet Five Minutes

A man of 60 has spent 20 years in bed and over three years in eating.

Arnold Bennett

Set aside half an hour every day to do all your worrying, then take a nap during this period.

Anon

I never take a nap after dinner but when I have had a bad night; and then the nap takes me.

Samuel Johnson

There is more refreshment and stimulation in a nap, even of the briefest, than in all the alcohol ever distilled.

Ovid

A nap, my friend, is a brief period of sleep which overtakes superannuated persons when they endeavour to entertain unwelcome visitors or to listen to scientific lectures.

George Bernard Shaw

I catnap now and then, but I think while I nap, so it's not a waste of time.

Martha Stewart

60! Now is the time to make your mark on the world – explore the Antarctic or become an astronaut. Make your mind up to take on exciting new challenges – straight after your afternoon nap.

Anon

Every businessman over 50 should have a daily nap and nip; a short nap after lunch and a relaxing highball before dinner.

Dr. Sara Murray Jordan

I have left orders to be awakened at any time in case of national emergency, even if I'm in a cabinet meeting.

Ronald Reagan

Menopausal Moments

YOU KNOW YOU'RE MENOPAUSAL WHEN…

…you're adding chocolate chips to your cheese omelette.

…the dryer has shrunk every last pair of your jeans.

…everyone around you has an attitude problem.

…your husband is suddenly agreeing to everything you say.

Menopausal Moments

…you're using your cellular phone to dial up every bumper sticker that says 'How's my driving – call 1-800-★★★-.'

…everyone's head looks like an invitation to batting practice.

…you're convinced there's a God and he's male.

…you can't believe they don't make a tampon bigger than Super Plus.

…you're sure that everyone is scheming to drive you crazy.

…the ibuprofen bottle is empty and you bought it yesterday.

All Anonymous

Male menopause is a lot more fun than female menopause. With female menopause you gain weight and get hot flashes. Male menopause – you get to date young girls and drive motorcycles.

Rita Rudner

I do get hot. Sometimes I think, 'Oh I can smell the menopause on me.' You know, it's kind of BO and Prozac and furniture polish.

Jenny Eclair, Grumpy Old Women

My first day as a woman and I am already having hot flushes.

Robin Williams, Mrs. Doubtfire

Middle-aged men are fine if they accept that they're middle-aged men. In fact, they're rather interesting when they accept that they're middle-aged men. But when they decide that they're going to act as if they're 19 or 20, and dress in a style that is inappropriate to that age, then it really is pathetic.

Ann Widdecombe, Grumpy Old Women

Rock and menopause do not mix. It is not good, it sucks and every day I fight it to the death, or, at the very least, not let it take me over.

Stevie Nicks

Charlotte: Listen to this: sometime in the ten years before menopause, you may experience symptoms including all-month-long PMS, fluid retention, insomnia, depression, hot flashes or irregular periods.
Carrie: On the plus side, people start to give up their seats for you on the bus.

Sex and the City

Inevitably I'm being given a hard time for being a typical ageing male, going off and packing in the wife.

Rick Stein

The Cracks of Time

For my sister's fiftieth birthday, I sent her a singing mammogram.

Steven Wright

I'm out of oestrogen and I've got a gun!

Bumper Sticker

The seven dwarves of menopause; itchy, bitchy, sweaty, sleepy, bloated, forgetful and psycho.

Anon

I'm developing a new fondness for Michael Douglas, now that he's getting all menopausal and wrinkly.

John Patterson

I certainly hope I'm not still answering child-star questions by the time I reach menopause.

Christina Ricci

The Cracks of Time

FADING LOOKS

How pleasant is the day when we give up striving to be young – or slender.

William James

The Cracks of Time

Most women are not as young as they are painted.

Max Beerbohm

My face looks like a wedding cake left out in the rain.

W.H. Auden

As we get older, our bodies get shorter and our anecdotes get longer.

Robert Quillen

I guess I look like a rock quarry that someone has dynamited.

Charles Bronson

Like a lot of fellows around here, I have a furniture problem. My chest has fallen into my drawers.

Billy Casper

If a woman tells you she's 20 and looks 16, she's 12. If she tells you she's 26 and looks 26, she's damn near 40.

Chris Rock

Robert Redford used to be such a handsome man and now look at him: everything has dropped, expanded and turned a funny colour.

George Best

The Cracks of Time

The outer passes away; the innermost is the same yesterday, today, and forever.

Thomas Carlyle

Many of my contemporaries have terrible feet, deformed by bunions, permanent corns and layers of dead skin like rock strata.

Sue Townsend

The problem with beauty is that it's like being born rich and getting poorer.

Joan Collins

Time may be a great healer, but it's a lousy beautician.

Lucille S. Harper

I ain't what I used to be, but who the hell is?

Dizzy Dean

I spent seven hours in a beauty shop – and that was just for the estimate.

Phyllis Diller

Take my photograph? You might as well use a picture of a relief map of Ireland!

Nancy Astor

I have a face like the behind of an elephant.

Charles Laughton

The Cracks of Time

Naked, I had a body that invited burial.

Spike Milligan

One day you look in the mirror and you realise that the face you are shaving is your father's.

Robert Harris

Some people, no matter how old they get, never lose their beauty – they merely move it from their faces into their hearts.

Martin Buxbaum

When I look in the mirror I don't see a rock star any more. I see a little balding old guy who looks like someone's uncle.

Pete Townshend

Wrinkles should merely indicate where smiles have been.

Mark Twain

You know you're getting fat when you can pinch an inch on your forehead.

John Mendoza

People say that age is just a state of mind. I say it's more about the state of your body.

Geoffrey Parfitt

The Cracks of Time

Time wounds all heels.

Groucho Marx

I have a face that is a cross between two pounds of halibut and an explosion in an old clothes closet.

David Niven

I look just like the girl next door… if you happen to live next to an amusement park.

Dolly Parton

Old age is when the liver spots show through your gloves.

Phyllis Diller

A man's as old as he's feeling. A woman as old as she looks.

Mortimer Collins

The excesses of our youth are cheques written against our age and they are payable with interest 30 years later.

Charles Caleb Colton

Looking 50 is great – if you're 60.

Joan Rivers

At age 50, everyone has the face he deserves.

George Orwell

The Cracks of Time

At 50, you have the choice of keeping your face or your figure and it's much better to keep your face.

Barbara Cartland

Anatomically speaking, a bust is here today and gone tomorrow.

Isobel Barnett

He must have had a magnificent build before his stomach went in for a career of its own.

Margaret Halsey

Muscles come and go; flab lasts.

Bill Vaughan

You can only perceive real beauty in a person as they get older.

Anouk Aimée

Men become much more attractive when they start looking older. But it doesn't do much for women, though we do have an advantage: make-up.

Bette Davis

Intellectual blemishes, like facial ones, grow more prominent with age.

François de La Rochefoucauld

The Cracks of Time

I'd like to change my butt. It hangs a little too long.
God forbid what it will look like when I'm older.
It will probably be dragging along on the ground
behind me.

Teri Hatcher

I'm tired of all this nonsense about beauty being
only skin-deep. That's deep enough. What do you
want – an adorable pancreas?

Jean Kerr

I don't believe make-up and the right hairstyle
alone can make a woman beautiful. The most
radiant woman in the room is the one full of life
and experience.

Sharon Stone

If you want to look young and thin, hang around
old fat people.

Jim Eason

Thank God for beauty products because at least
they give you hope. Even if they do nothing for
you, you can sort of slam the box to your forehead
and think it's helping. And it has to be expensive
stuff because if it's cheap stuff, it won't work. I'm
not interested in cheap stuff. I don't care if it's all
packaging, that's fine by me. Just as long as it sells
me a dream.

Nina Myskow, Grumpy Old Women

The Cracks of Time

It's time we stopped worrying about losing our looks and started celebrating the gifts of age: I feel yummier than ever.

Sela Ward

I am sitting here thinking how nice it is that wrinkles don't hurt.

Anon

I don't think age is an ugly process. I think age is a beautiful thing. I love wrinkles. I don't like falling down. If I just wrinkle, I may not touch. If I fall down, I'll lift up.

Linda Evangelista

A beautiful lady is an accident of nature. A beautiful old lady is a work of art.

Louis Nizer

When you have loved as she has loved, you grow old beautifully.

W. Somerset Maugham

Midlife has hit you when you stand naked in front of a mirror and can see your rear end without turning around!

Anon

The older I get, the more I feel almost beautiful.

Sharon Olds

The Cracks of Time

I guess I don't so much mind being old, as I mind being fat and old.

Peter Gabriel

You can take no credit for beauty at 16. But if you are beautiful at 60, it will be your own soul's doing.

Marie Stopes

It really costs me a lot emotionally to watch myself on-screen. I think of myself, and feel like I'm quite young, and then I look at this old man with the baggy chins and the tired eyes and the receding hairline and all that.

Gene Hackman

Midlife is when the growth of the hair on our legs slows down. This gives us plenty of time to care for our newly acquired moustache.

Anon

Middle age is when your wife tells you to pull in your stomach, and you already have.

Jack Barry

I am going to carry on colouring my hair, wearing diamonds and painting my nails until the day I die.

Jenni Murray

The Cracks of Time

Liza Minnelli looks like a very old 13.

Jonathan Ross

Midlife women no longer have upper arms, we have wingspans. We are no longer women in sleeveless shirts; we are flying squirrels in drag.

Anon

I think that the longer I look good, the better gay men feel.

Cher

It's okay to be fat. So you're fat. Just be fat and shut up about it.

Roseanne Barr

It's simple, if it jiggles it's fat.

Arnold Schwarzenegger

The older you get, the tougher it is to lose weight, because by then your body and your fat are really good friends.

Anon

If I had been around when Rubens was painting, I would have been revered as a fabulous model. Kate Moss? Well, she would have been the paintbrush.

Dawn French

The Cracks of Time

I'm going to have wrinkles really soon.

Cher

Character contributes to beauty. It fortifies a woman as her youth fades.

Jacqueline Bisset

In middle life, the human back is spoiling for a technical knockout and will use the flimsiest excuse, even a sneeze, to fall apart.

Elwyn Brooks White

Brilliantly lit from stem to stern, she looked like a sagging birthday cake.

Walter Lord

Even with all my wrinkles! I am beautiful!

Edward Everett Hale

Wear a smile and have friends; wear a scowl and have wrinkles.

George Eliot

Well, her face was so wrinkled it looked like seven miles of bad road.

W.C. Fields

Folding Back the Years

COSMETIC SURGERY

I want to grow old without facelifts. I want to have the courage to be loyal to the face I have made.

Marilyn Monroe

I'd make plastic surgery compulsory for every woman over 40.

Simon Cowell

My husband said 'show me your boobs' and I had to pull up my skirt… so it was time to get them done!

Dolly Parton

Please don't retouch my wrinkles. It took me so long to earn them.

Anna Magnani

A plastic surgeon's office is the only place where no one gets offended when you pick your nose.

MAD Magazine

I don't suggest that her face has been lifted, but there's a possibility that her body has been lowered.

Clive James

Folding Back the Years

The only parts left of my original body are my elbows.

Phyllis Diller

Look at Cher. One more face lift and she'll be wearing a beard.

Jennifer Saunders

Sylvester Stallone's mother's plastic surgery looks so bad it could have been bought through a mail order catalogue.

Graham Norton

I don't need plastic surgery. I need Lourdes.

Paul O'Grady

Why fear terrorists? With treatments like botox, women are waging germ warfare on themselves at £250 a pop.

Kathy Lette

If anybody says their facelift doesn't hurt, they're lying. It was like I'd spent the night with an axe murderer.

Sharon Osbourne

I was going to have cosmetic surgery until I noticed that the doctor's office was full of portraits by Picasso.

Rita Rudner

My Aching Bones!

HEALTH

First the doctor told me the good news: I was going to have a disease named after me.

Steve Martin

My father died of cancer when I was a teenager. He had it before it became popular.

Goodman Ace

You know you're getting old when everything hurts. And what doesn't hurt doesn't work.

Hy Gardner

The trouble with heart disease is that the first symptom is often hard to deal with – sudden death.

Michael Phelps

I am afraid… that health begins, after 70, and often long before, to have a meaning different from that which it had at 30. But it is culpable to murmur at the established order of the creation, as it is vain to oppose it. He that lives, must grow old; and he that would rather grow old than die, has God to thank for the infirmities of old age.

Samuel Johnson

My Aching Bones!

My doctor gave me six months to live, but when I couldn't pay the bill he gave me six more.

Walter Matthau

Life begins at 40 – but so do fallen arches, rheumatism, faulty eyesight, and the tendency to tell a story to the same person, three or four times.

William Feather

As the arteries grow hard, the heart grows soft.

Henry Louis Mencken

Nobody expects to trust his body overmuch after the age of 50.

Edward Hoagland

The trouble about always trying to preserve the health of the body is that it is so difficult to do without destroying the health of the mind.

G.K. Chesterton

Two elderly gentlemen from a retirement centre were sitting on a bench under a tree when one turned to the other and said, 'Ted, I'm 83 years old now and I'm just full of aches and pains. I know you're about my age. How do you feel?'

Ted said, 'I feel like a newborn baby.'

'Really? Like a newborn baby?'

'Yep. No hair, no teeth, and I think I just wet my pants.'

Anon

I drive way too fast to worry about cholesterol.

Steven Wright

We all get heavier as we get older because there is a lot more information in our heads.

Vlade Divac

The spiritual eyesight improves as the physical eyesight declines.

Plato

Don't you think it's unnerving that doctors call what they do 'Practice'?

George Carlin

Quit worrying about your health. It'll go away.

Robert Orben

Each year it grows harder to make ends meet – the ends I refer to are hands and feet.

Richard Armour

It's no longer a question of staying healthy. It's a question of finding a sickness you like.

Jackie Mason

My Aching Bones!

A woman walked up to a little old man rocking in a chair on his porch.

'I couldn't help noticing how happy you look,' she said. 'What's your secret for a long happy life?'

'I smoke three packs of cigarettes a day,' he said. 'I also drink a case of whisky a week, eat fatty foods, and never exercise.'

'That's amazing,' the woman said. 'How old are you?'

'26,' he said.

Anon

Never under any circumstances take a sleeping pill and a laxative on the same night.

Dave Barry

So who's perfect? Washington had false teeth. Franklin was nearsighted. Mussolini had syphilis. Unpleasant things have been said about Walt Whitman and Oscar Wilde. Tchaikovsky had his problems, too. And Lincoln was constipated.

John O'Hara

I have finally come to the conclusion that a good reliable set of bowels is worth more to man than any quantity of brains.

Josh Billings

My Aching Bones!

My grandfather is hard of hearing. He needs to read lips. I don't mind him reading lips, but he uses one of those yellow highlighters.

Brian Kiley

A man does not die of love or his liver or even of old age; he dies of being a man.

Percival Arland Ussher

I think most people would pick sudden heart attack and in sleep. We assume that's the best way to die, because you never know.

Jack Kevorkian

There are only three things that can kill a farmer: lightning, rolling over in a tractor, and old age.

Bill Bryson

For years I was an undiagnosed anorexic, suffering from a little-known variant of the disease, where, freakishly, the appetite turns in on itself and demands more and more food, forcing the sufferer to gain several stones in weight and wear men's V-necked pullovers. My condition has stabilised now, but I can never stray too far from cocoa-based products and I keep a small cracknel-type candy in my brassiere at all times. Fortunately, I wear a 'D' cup so there is plenty of room for sweetmeats...

Victoria Wood

I feel stronger, but physically I feel like I'm falling apart. Every day I get a new pain or ache and think, 'Oh, that will be a hip replacement in a couple of years!'

Yasmin Le Bon

Money cannot buy health, but I'd settle for a diamond-studded wheelchair.

Dorothy Parker

I think that in youth you never view an ailment as possibly fatal. When you get an ailment in middle age, you are automatically planning your own funeral...

Will Self

I have such poor vision I can date anybody.

Garry Shandling

Doctor, Doctor

THE MEDICAL PROFESSION

In the name of Hippocrates, doctors have invented the most exquisite form of torture ever known to man: survival.

Luis Buñuel

Doctor, Doctor

Cured yesterday of my disease, I died last night of
my physician.

Matthew Prior

The medics can now stretch life out an additional
dozen years but they don't tell you that most of
these years are going to be spent flat on your back
while some ghoul with thick glasses and a matted
skull peers at you through a machine that's hot out
of 'Space Patrol'.

Groucho Marx

Beware of the young doctor and the old barber.

Benjamin Franklin

The doctor called Mrs. Cohen saying, 'Mrs. Cohen,
your cheque came back.' Mrs. Cohen answered, 'So
did my arthritis!' The doctor says, 'You'll live to be
60!' 'I AM 60!' 'See, what did I tell you?'

Henny Youngman

Too many good docs are getting out of the business.
Too many OB-GYNs aren't able to practise their love
with women all across this country.

George W. Bush

My doctor is wonderful. Once, in 1955, when I
couldn't afford an operation, he touched up the X-
rays.

Joey Bishop

Doctor, Doctor

After two days in hospital, I took a turn for the nurse.

W.C. Fields

Doctors are the same as lawyers; the only difference is that lawyers merely rob you, whereas doctors rob you and kill you too.

Anton Chekhov

One of the most difficult things to contend with in a hospital is that assumption on the part of the staff that because you have lost your gall bladder you have also lost your mind.

Jean Kerr

Keep away from physicians. It is all probing and guessing and pretending with them. They leave it to Nature to cure in her own time, but they take the credit. As well as very fat fees.

Anthony Burgess

My doctor tells me I'm in very good nick. The most positive way to think about death is to try to live.

Michael Caine

The ultimate indignity is to be given a bedpan by a stranger who calls you by your first name.

Maggie Kuhn

Doctor, Doctor

I'm not feeling very well, I need a doctor immediately. Ring the nearest golf course.

Groucho Marx

Thanks to modern medicine we are no longer forced to endure prolonged pain, disease, discomfort and wealth.

Robert Orben

At my age, every doctor says the same thing; it's either something I have to live with – or something I have to live without.

Anon

Never go to a doctor whose office plants have died.

Erma Bombeck

My doctor gave me two weeks to live. I hope they are in August.

Ronnie Shakes

Our doctor would never really operate unless it was necessary. He was just that way. If he didn't need the money, he wouldn't lay a hand on you.

Herb Shriner

My doctor once said to me, 'Do you think I'm here for the good of your health?'

Bob Monkhouse

Doctor, Doctor

America's health care system is second only to Japan... Canada, Sweden, Great Britain... well, all of Europe. But you can thank your lucky stars we don't live in Paraguay!

Homer Simpson

A hospital bed is a parked taxi, with the meter running.

Groucho Marx

A woman tells her doctor, 'I've got a bad back.' The doctor says, 'It's old age.' The woman says, 'I want a second opinion.' The doctor says: 'Okay – you're ugly as well.'

Tommy Cooper

My kid could get a bad X-ray and I could get a call from the doctor saying I have something growing in my bum and that would change my perspective on everything instantaneously, on what is and what is not important.

Tom Hanks

I've wrestled with reality for 35 years, and I'm happy, Doctor, I finally won out over it.

Jimmy Stewart, Harvey

Dick Cheney said he was running again. He said his health was fine, 'I've got a doctor with me 24 hours a day.' Yeah, that's always the sign of a man in good health, isn't it?

David Letterman

I kept thinking about that large doctor, sweaty, who brought my mother home after the first heart attack. He said, 'Don't ever get angry at your mother, that might kill her.' That set off my demons, I think.

Gene Wilder

I told the doctor I broke my leg in two places. He told me to quit going to those places.

Henny Youngman

Dad always thought laughter was the best medicine, which I guess is why several of us died of tuberculosis.

Jack Handey

I don't know why people question the academic training of an athlete. 50 per cent of the doctors in this country graduated in the bottom half of their classes.

Al McGuire

When I go in for a physical, they no longer ask how old I am. They just carbon-date me.

Ronald Reagan

You Know You're Getting Old When...

There's a new medical crisis. Doctors are reporting that many men are having allergic reactions to latex condoms. They say they cause severe swelling. So what's the problem?

Dustin Hoffman

I know of nothing more laughable than a doctor who does not die of old age.

Voltaire

On a Friday night it's like a field hospital in the Battle of the Somme. There's blokes with blood coming out of their heads and Bacardi Breezer bottles stuck in their necks.

John O'Farrell, on A&E departments in Grumpy Old Men

You Know You're Getting Old When...

...the only thing you want for your birthday is not to be reminded of it.

...'Happy Hour' turns out to be a nap!

...it takes you all night to do what you used to do all night!

You Know You're Getting Old When...

...you sink your teeth into an apple and they stay there!

...your back goes out more often than you do!

...you can't get your rocking chair started!

...it feels like the morning after and you haven't been anywhere.

...you get winded playing chess.

...being a little hippie does not have the same meaning as it did in the 60s.

...everything either dries up or leaks.

...you go for a mammogram and you realise it is the only time someone will ever ask you to appear topless in a film.

...your wife gives up sex for Lent, and you don't know till the 4th of July.

All Anonymous

...you've lost all your marvels.

Merry Browne

...you walk into a record store and everything you like has been marked down to $1.99.

Jack Simmons

…All the names in your black book have M.D. after them.

Arnold Palmer

…The candles cost more than the cake.

George Burns

The Good Old Days

MEMORIES

Nothing is more responsible for the good old days than a bad memory.

Franklin P. Adams

When I was young I was called a rugged individualist. When I was in my 50s I was considered eccentric. Here I am doing and saying the same things I did then and I'm labelled senile.

George Burns

We have all passed a lot of water since then.

Samuel Goldwyn

The one thing I remember about Christmas was that my father used to take me out in a boat about 10 miles offshore on Christmas Day, and I used to have to swim back. Extraordinary. It was a ritual.

Mind you, that wasn't the hard part. The difficult bit was getting out of the sack.

John Cleese

When you finally go back to your old home town, you find it wasn't the old home you missed but your childhood.

Sam Ewing

The older you get, the more you tell it like it used to be.

Anon

When I was a boy, the Dead Sea was only sick.

George Burns

When I was a kid my parents moved a lot, but I always found them.

Rodney Dangerfield

I was so naive as a kid I used to sneak behind the barn and do nothing.

Johnny Carson

Most people like the old days best – they were younger then.

Anon

I can remember when the air was clean and sex was dirty.

George Burns

The Good Old Days

There's a lot to do when you're a kid – spiders to catch, girls to poke in the eye – stuff to be getting on with.

Alan Davies

I remember when I was seven, sitting backstage in Vegas while these topless showgirls adjusted their G-strings in front of me. It was a strange way to grow up.

Donny Osmond

Nostalgia, the vice of the aged. We watch so many old movies our memories come in monochrome.

Angela Carter

The older a man gets, the farther he had to walk to school as a boy.

Anon

In every age 'the good old days' were a myth. No one ever thought they were good at the time. For every age has consisted of crises that seemed intolerable to the people who lived through them.

Brooks Atkinson

Nostalgia is a file that removes the rough edges from the good old days.

Doug Larson

We seem to be going through a period of nostalgia, and everyone seems to think yesterday was better than today. I don't think it was, and I would advise you not to wait 10 years before admitting today was great. If you're hung up on nostalgia, pretend today is yesterday and just go out and have one hell of a time

Art Buchwald

You don't appreciate a lot of stuff in school until you get older. Little things like being spanked every day by a middle-aged woman: stuff you pay good money for in later life.

Emo Philips

What's in An Age?

It is so comic to hear oneself called old, even at 90, I suppose!

Alice James

Age puzzles me. I thought it was a quiet time. My 70s were interesting and fairly serene, but my 80s are passionate. I grow more intense as I age.

Florida Scott-Maxwell

The hardest years in life are those between 10 and 70.

Helen Hayes

What's in An Age?

There's one advantage to being 102. No peer pressure.

Dennis Wolfberg

People under 24 think old age starts around 55, those over 75, on the other hand, believe that youth doesn't end until the age of 58.

Alexander Chancellor

I'm 65 and I guess that puts me in with the geriatrics. But if there were 15 months in every year, I'd only be 48. That's the trouble with us. We number everything. Take women, for example. I think they deserve to have more than 12 years between the ages of 28 and 40.

James Thurber

No one is so old as to think he cannot live one more year.

Marcus T. Cicero

No woman should ever be quite accurate about her age. It looks so calculating.

Oscar Wilde

Who wants to be 95? 94-year-olds.

George Burns

The age of a woman doesn't mean a thing. The best tunes are played on the oldest fiddles.

Ralph Waldo Emerson

What's in An Age?

Autumn is really the best of seasons; and I'm not sure that old age isn't the best part of life.

C.S. Lewis

I'm not interested in age. People who tell me their age are silly. You're as old as you feel.

Elizabeth Arden

Like many women my age, I am 28 years old.

Mary Schmitt

The seven ages of man: spills, drills, thrills, bills, ills, pills and wills.

Richard John Needham

How the hell should I know? Most of the people my age are dead.

Casey Stengel, on the subject of his age

Age ain't nothin' but a number. But age is other things too. It is wisdom, if one has lived one's life properly. It is experience and knowledge. And it is getting to know all the ways the world turns, so that if you cannot turn the world the way you want, you can at least get out of the way so you won't get run over.

Miriam Makeba

A sexagenarian? At his age? I think that's disgusting.

Gracie Allen

What's in An Age?

You can judge your age by the amount of pain you feel when you come in contact with a new idea.

John Nuveen

I do wish I could tell you my age but it's impossible. It keeps changing all the time.

Greer Garson

I am luminous with age.

Meridel Le Sueur

Age is not measured by years. Nature does not equally distribute energy. Some people are born old and tired while others are going strong at 70.

Dorothy Thompson

Your 50s are mature, reliable and dependable – or boring, predictable and conventional.

T. Kinnes

Old age is a special problem for me because I've never been able to shed the mental image I have of myself – a lad of about 19.

E.B. White

I'm 57. I can't look like a 30-year-old. You try to hold age at bay, but there comes a point when you just have to give up gracefully.

Elton John

What's in An Age?

The biggest disadvantage of old age is that you can't outgrow it.

Anon

Old age brings along with its uglinesses the comfort that you will soon be out of it – which ought to be a substantial relief to such discontented pendulums as we are.

Ralph Waldo Emerson

You can calculate Zsa Zsa Gabor's age by the rings on her fingers.

Bob Hope

At 65 and drawing a state pension, I was delighted to discover that only people under 45 would regard me as old, even though sadly nobody would actually call me young.

Alexander Chancellor

Nobody knows the age of the human race, but everybody agrees that it is old enough to know better.

Anon

Age is whatever you think it is. You are as old as you think you are.

Muhammad Ali

Writing the Memoirs

When you get to my age you either run away or jump in with both feet.

Jan Leeming

I think all this talk about age is foolish. Every time I'm one year older, everyone else is too.

Gloria Swanson

Age is not a handicap. Age is nothing but a number. It is how you use it.

Diesel Payne

Nobody grows old by merely living a number of years. People grow old only by deserting their ideals. Years wrinkle the face, but to give up enthusiasm wrinkles the soul.

Anon

Age is just a number. It's totally irrelevant unless, of course, you happen to be a bottle of wine.

Joan Collins

Writing the Memoirs

Keep a diary, and someday it'll keep you.

Mae West

Writing the Memoirs

I was born because it was a habit in those days, people didn't know anything else.

Will Rogers

My father had a profound influence on me, he was a lunatic.

Spike Milligan

I used to think I was an interesting person, but I must tell you how sobering a thought it is to realise your life's story fills about 35 pages and you have, actually, not much to say.

Roseanne Barr

I wanted to be president of the United States. I really did. The older I get, the less preposterous the idea seems.

Alec Baldwin

Thank goodness I was never sent to school: it would have rubbed off some of the originality.

Beatrix Potter

I succeeded by saying what everyone else is thinking.

Joan Rivers

I wrote the story myself. It's about a girl who lost her reputation and never missed it.

Mae West

Writing the Memoirs

Each has his past shut in him like the leaves of a book known to him by his heart, and his friends can only read the title.

Virginia Woolf

When I was growing up, there were two things that were unpopular in my house. One was me, and the other was my guitar.

Bruce Springsteen

I wasn't as smart then as I am now. But who ever is?

Tina Turner

When I realised what I had turned out to be was a lousy, two-bit pool hustler and a drunk, I wasn't depressed at all. I was glad to have a profession.

Danny McGoorty, Irish pool player

In my 20s, my pleasures tended to be physical. In my 30s, my pleasures tended to be intellectual. I can't say which was more exquisite.

Steve Kangas

I always wanted to be an explorer, but – it seemed I was doomed to be nothing more than a very silly person.

Michael Palin

Writing the Memoirs

I have never described the time I was in *Doctor Who* as anything except a kind of ecstatic success, but all the rest has been rather a muddle and a disappointment. Compared to *Doctor Who*, it has been an outrageous failure really – it's so boring.

Tom Baker

I'm writing an unauthorized autobiography.

Steven Wright

I don't think anyone should write his autobiography until after he's dead.

Samuel Goldwyn

An autobiography is an obituary in serial form with the last instalment missing.

Quentin Crisp

Rebecca was a busy liar in her distinguished old age, reinventing her past for gullible biographers.

Walter Clemons, on Rebecca West

All I ever seemed to get was the kind of girl who had a special dispensation from Rome to wear the thickest part of her legs below the knee.

Hugh Leonard

I couldn't wait for success, so I went on ahead without it.

Jonathan Winters

Writing the Memoirs

I spent 90 per cent of my money on women and drink. The rest I wasted.

George Best

On what?
> *Chris Eubank*, when asked if he had ever thought of writing an autobiography

I always knew looking back on my tears would bring me laughter, but I never knew looking back on my laughter would make me cry.

Cat Stevens

Forty pictures I was in, and all I remember is 'What kind of bra will you be wearing today, honey?' That was always the area of big decision – from the neck to the navel.

Donna Reed

The really good idea is always traceable back quite a long way, often to a not very good idea which sparked off another idea that was only slightly better, which somebody else misunderstood in such a way that they then said something which was really rather interesting.

John Cleese

My toughest fight was with my first wife, and she won every round.

Muhammad Ali

Writing the Memoirs

It was no great tragedy being Judy Garland's daughter. I had tremendously interesting childhood years – except they had little to do with being a child.

Liza Minnelli

This is the second most bizarre thing ever to happen to me. The first was when I was sued by a woman who claimed she became pregnant because she watched me on TV and I bent her contraceptive coil.

Uri Geller

This bikini made me a success.

Ursula Andress

I wanted revenge; I wanted to dance on the graves of a few people who made me unhappy. It's a pretty infantile way to go through life – I'll show them – but I've done it, and I've got more than I ever dreamed of.

Anthony Hopkins

I sold the memoirs of my sex life to a publisher – they are going to make a board game out of it.

Woody Allen

I grew up in Europe, where the history comes from.

Eddie Izzard

Writing the Memoirs

I was coming home from kindergarten – well, they told me it was kindergarten. I found out later I had been working in a factory for ten years. It's good for a kid to know how to make gloves.

Ellen DeGeneres

Success didn't spoil me, I've always been insufferable.

Fran Lebowitz

My childhood was a period of waiting for the moment when I could send everyone and everything connected with it to hell.

Igor Stravinsky

I can't understand why I flunked American history. When I was a kid there was so little of it.

George Burns

There is nothing that makes you so aware of the improvisation of human existence as a song unfinished or an old address book.

Carson McCullers

I didn't really say everything I said.

Yogi Berra

It took me 15 years to discover I had no talent for writing, but I couldn't give it up, because by that time I was too famous.

Robert Benchley

Writing the Memoirs

History will be kind to me for I intend to write it.

Winston Churchill

There used to be a real me, but I had it surgically removed.

Peter Sellers

Acting is merely the art of keeping a large group of people from coughing.

Sir Ralph Richardson

As a kid, I knew I wanted to be either a cartoonist or an astronaut. The latter was never much of a possibility, as I don't even like riding in elevators.

Bill Watterson

The most important thing I would learn in school was that almost everything I would learn in school would be utterly useless. When I was 15 I knew the principal industries of the Ruhr Valley, the underlying causes of World War One and what Peig Sayers had for her dinner every day… What I wanted to know when I was 15 was the best way to chat up girls. That is what I still want to know.

Joseph O'Connor, The Secret World of the Irish Male

If I'd only known, I would have been a locksmith.

Albert Einstein

Famous Last Words

Bless you, Sister. May all your sons be bishops.

Brendan Behan

Why not? After all, it belongs to him.

Charlie Chaplin, after a priest said, 'May the Lord have mercy on your soul.'

Never felt better.

Douglas Fairbanks Snr.

I have offended God and mankind because my work did not reach the quality it should have.

Leonardo da Vinci

My wallpaper and I are fighting a duel to the death. One or the other of us has to go.

Oscar Wilde

This isn't *Hamlet*, you know, it's not meant to go into the bloody ear.

Laurence Olivier, to his nurse, who had spilt water on him

Dammit… Don't you dare ask God to help me.

Joan Crawford, after her housekeeper began to pray aloud

Famous Last Words

Why should I talk to you? I've just been talking to your boss.

> *Wilson Mizner,* to a priest standing over his bed

Born in a hotel room and, goddamn it, died in a hotel room.

> *Eugene O'Neill*

Drink to me!

> *Pablo Picasso*

God bless… God damn.

> *James Thurber*

Go away. I'm all right.

> *H. G. Wells*

Curtain! Fast music! Lights! Ready for the last finale! Great! The show looks good. The show looks good.

> *Florenz Ziegfeld,* Broadway producer

Die? I should say not, dear fellow. No Barrymore would allow such a conventional thing to happen to him.

> *John Barrymore*

Friends applaud, the comedy is finished.

> *Ludwig van Beethoven*

Famous Last Words

I am about to – or I am going to – die: either expression is correct.

> *Dominique Bouhours,* French grammarian

Goodnight, my darlings, I'll see you tomorrow.

> *Noel Coward*

Why do you weep? Did you think I was immortal?

> *Louis XIV,* King of France

Sister, you're trying to keep me alive as an old curiosity, but I'm done, I'm finished, I'm going to die.

> *George Bernard Shaw,* to his nurse

Oh, I am not going to die, am I? He will not separate us, we have been so happy.

> *Charlotte Brontë,* to her husband of nine months, Rev. Arthur Nicholls

I've had 18 straight whiskies, I think that's the record...

> *Dylan Thomas*

I should never have switched from Scotch to Martinis.

> *Humphrey Bogart*

I've had a hell of a lot of fun and I've enjoyed every minute of it.

> *Errol Flynn*